What did Cap Brown do for Ecology?

The legacy for biodiversity, landscapes, and nature conservation

Edited by Ian D. Rotherham and Christine Handley

British Ecological Society
Forest Ecology Group

Sheffield Hallam University

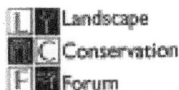

Landscape
Conservation
Forum

Historic England

300 years
Capability
Brown

Edited by Ian D. Rotherham and Christine Handley

Published by:

Wildtrack Publishing, Venture House,
103 Arundel Street, Sheffield S1 2NT

Typeset and processed by Christine Handley

Supported by:

British Ecological Society Forest Ecology Special Interest Group.
HEC Associates.
Historic England
IUFRO.
Landscape Conservation Forum.
Sheffield Hallam University.
South Yorkshire Biodiversity Research Group.

ISBN: 978-1-904098-65-2

ISSN: 1354-0262

Contents

Shorter contributions

Foreword

This book is based on a major conference with Historic England, Natural England, the Ancient Tree Forum and others which took place in 2016 as part of the celebrations for the tercentenary of Lancelot 'Capability' Brown. The event brought together ecologists, landscape historians and archaeologists, land managers and conservationists to look critically at the impact of Brown and his successors on the UK's landscape.

The book addresses the paradigms of these designed landscapes. It considers the issues around the legacy of Brown's creations and ideas and the repercussions that are still apparent today. It makes for a thought-provoking and rich discussion covering habitat conservation and creation, drainage and the release of alien species. This is the untold story of the ecology of Capability Brown and the landscape school which followed.

Ian D. Rotherham
May 2017

What did Capability Brown do for Ecology?

Ian D. Rotherham

Sheffield Hallam University

Figure 1. Lancelot 'Capability' Brown (1715-1783)

Summary

Lancelot Brown, more commonly 'Capability' Brown, was an English landscape architect, designer, and artist. However, most of the build-up to 2016 and the extensive media coverage and interest so far, has focused, and indeed will focus, on Brown's legacy of landscaped parks and gardens, the settings for great houses. Not much has been said about the impacts of Brown and of his followers on British ecology. Indeed, there has been only limited research done on this aspect of the English landscape school. In terms of the ecology of parks such as the 'Brown' landscapes, there is little known of their past ecologies. Furthermore, it is only relatively recently that contemporary value has been recognised in terms of veteran trees, associated invertebrates, and mammals such as bats. The wider ecosystem functioning and the 'hidden' ecology of mycorrhizal and saprophytic fungi for example, remains elusive. We know little of what preceded Brown and therefore it is hard to pin down the impacts of his sweeping influence in the British landscape. However, Brown in his planting schemes and those that followed, both his supporters and those less enthused by his vision, began a great change in ecology towards what we see today, a landscape of 'recombinant' and 'hybrid' communities. To date, this watershed in British eco-history has remained largely unnoticed.

There are key questions to be asked, in particular:

1. What did Brown and his followers protect?
2. What did Brown and his followers destroy, remove, or replace?
3. What was Brown's influence in and throughout the wider landscape?
4. What might be the future ecologies of these landscapes?

To address these issues and questions requires a multi-disciplinary approach, something which many universities seem to find hard to deliver in the research silos of the funding council environment. In order to understand the impacts of Brown and his school, we need to bring together the work of historian, garden and landscape historians, archaeologists, historical economists, ecologists, entomologists and tree historians. Then, through collaborative studies in the wider landscape context and detailed individual case studies of sites, and their longitudinal time-lines, we can begin to evaluate the Brown effect. Trees, herbs, and insects for example, can inform the changes over time to demonstrate continuity or severance in the parkland landscape. Garden and landscape histories can be combined with ecological work to show how species ebbed and flowed in the eighteenth and nineteenth centuries. Maps and plans can show ancient trees removed or retained, and the entomologists can assess the species present today in order to join science to history in a broader understanding. Account books and plans can illustrate the physical impacts of the landscapers in transforming or conserving nature and countryside. Such insights can then help inform future plans for these important landscapes.

Introduction

Figure 2. Clumber Park House, Nottinghamshire

The impacts of the English landscape movement, for which Brown was a major innovator and influence, operate through social, economic, political processes and relate to changes in all of these. The results of the Brownian landscapers have consequences for future changes in the countryside, for landscape perceptions, for ecology and more. One major observation to emerge from the study of the Brown phenomenon is the widespread decision by wealthy, private landowners to move landscapes from productive agricultural options towards grand vistas and what might be described as 'tame wildernesses'. Perhaps here we see a link to the emergence of newly 'wilded' landscape such as at Knepp Castle in West Sussex. In terms of addressing current environmental crises and envisioning a future and richer landscape / countryside, might private landowners once again be persuaded to offset some profit against long-term, wider legacy? Additionally, could the publicly-funded grant-aid system be harnessed to help deliver this?

For example, could the great and the good be persuaded once again, to 'wild' the English landscape? Furthermore, if these created wild-sites could be financially viable, then landowners might just take such ideas seriously. In this context, it is worth noting that we lack any over-arching assessments of the economic worth of today's (very significant) Brownian landscapes or of their tourism impacts. This is despite requests for support to gather vital data on economic functions and impacts, and which to date have fallen on deaf ears, would provide political argument to drive forward a positive conservation agenda.

In terms of understanding the ecological impacts of the Brown phenomenon, it is important to place Brown in the context of his time, and of the gardeners and landscapers who were his contemporaries, his predecessors, and his followers. Also, and hugely influential were the powerful landowners who commissioned the great designers and gardeners to reflect their own passions, philosophies, and politics. Brown's influence was not that of a single individual but more like the waves created by throwing a rock into a pond so that they interact, buffet, and wash over one another. Some waves have more impact than others, and some are transformed into longer-term under-currents. So Kent and Bridgeman preceded and influenced Brown, and Uvedale Price, Richard Payne Knight, Repton followed. Repton (1752-1818) perhaps more than the others, carried forwards the Brown ideas; Price and Knight were his most vociferous critics. Joseph Paxton and others were also influential, especially at particular sites such as Chatsworth in Derbyshire, and William Robinson (1838-1935) influenced the wider garden landscape and the urban parks movement as they evolved and emerged throughout the 1800s.

Improvement

Figure 3. Holkham Hall, Norfolk

When we consider the influences of Brown, his predecessors and followers, we must place this analysis within a context of 'improvement' and 'enclosure', of 'drainage' and 'reclamation', of 'urbanisation', of globalisation', and 'modernisation'. At the time of the creation of many of Brown's great visions, the

English countryside in particular was already being traumatised by dramatic changes on a scale never previously witnessed. The common was wrested from the commoner and the countryside was being depopulated by migration to urban sweat-shops. Outside the park pale, the landscape was being intensified and improved as an agricultural factory. Within the park pale, funded by agricultural improvement and early industrialisation, the land was to be transformed to a leisurely landscape for the benefit of the great and the good.

Helpful in terms of research on specific sites is the fact that Brown kept his 'Red Books' of notes on sites and projects. However, whilst these may capture and detail ideas and visions, it is also clear that we often do not know the specifics of what precisely came to pass, and indeed, who did it. Sometimes the estate garden took charge, and other times one of Brown's employees. In many cases the estate owner appears to have been influential. Then of course, there were the impacts of the landscapers, gardeners, and owners that followed through nearly three hundred years to the present day.

Figure 4. Holkham Hall monument to Thomas Coke

Within the park

Essentially, before modern agri-industrial processes and impacts, the results for ecology of major landscape changes in the countryside are not clear-cut. Furthermore, in order to gauge ecological impacts, it is important to have an understanding of the dynamic and fluid nature of landscape and its ecology combined with the role of continuity through time and space (see Rotherham, 2014 for example). In attempts to consider historical ecology, these basic elements are often omitted or at least, poorly understood. Additionally, it is worth considering that in a pre-industrial, pre-petrochemical age, landscape transformations are neither as complete nor as rigorous as they might be today. Essentially, species and propagules can hang on in safe areas to re-colonise when conditions once again become suitable. This is what Barry Wright and I have described as the 'grubby landscape' phenomenon and it allows many plans for example, to pass down through centuries as they ebb and flow, flux and change in the landscape setting.

Figure 5: Holkham Hall, Norfolk with design by Kent and a Brown plan never implemented though Brown may have implemented or amended some of Kent's designs

Therefore, the consequence of even major transformations such as the imposition of Brownian parks is actually of a 'grubby' landscape in which species survive to re-colonise the new park and its ecological opportunities. Thus, we see so-called ecological indicators of old or ancient landscapes reappearing after imparkation in largely secondary habitats. Over centuries, in a pre-industrial and less fragmented countryside, species are able to move more effectively and freely that we witness today. To understand the Brown ecology we must consider it within this 'pre-improvement' context.

Figure 6: Bluebell an ancient landscape indicator moving slowly in a 'grubby' landscape

Furthermore, although these landscapes were transformed by the landscape designers they were often only moderately 'improved'. This means that these plants and animals that are generally stress-tolerators and stress-tolerant ruderals are able to re-establish quite quickly and we see a dynamic process of species acquisition over time after the imparkation. Some species survive and others re-colonise. Importantly for current and future ecologies and for nature conservation particularly, veteran trees were often enclosed within the park and safeguarded. Beyond the pale, they were generally lost at a later date. However, there were removals too as some trees were ruthlessly removed to create vistas or other landscape effects. Overall, the park environment may have provided important ecological continuity and protection for certain selected features.

Within the parkland landscape, the habitat creation of Brown and others often related to the management of water. On the one hand, they desiccated wet landscapes, destroying unique and important habitats, and on the other hand they created ponds, lakes and other features now of value as feeding habitats to bats which roost and breed in the veteran, hollow trees. Brown both created water features but drained wetlands and modified rivers; on the one hand creating new habitats and on the other destroying or modifying existing ones. Similarly, he retained some veteran trees, but removed others; and he planted parkland standard trees, plus mounds and roundels of plantation woods, and extensive roadside avenues.

The expansive grasslands so typical of 'Brownian School' parks are often relatively 'unimproved' yet at the same time species-poor in flowering plants. This poverty may reflect often-intensive grazing regimes over long periods but also origins in some cases from one-time arable lands. The older ecologies show through the more recent veneer of the landscaped park. Because we frequently know little of the ecology pre-Brown, it is hard to judge the dynamics of what has happened since. However, the landscape taken in to the park must have had a huge influence of what survived and what evolved.

Clearly, the origins of the landscape park ecology vary with location and the specific history and time-line of what was taken into the parkland and its subsequent management. In some landscape parks, there may be direct links back to a much older deer park, and when this is the case, then the ecology may be uniquely exciting and provide genuine continuity to an ancient countryside. However, we again know relatively little of the real-time ecology of such areas. These ancient parks were much more functional productive landscapes than the ornamental parks of Brown's affluent clients. They were recreational countryside in terms of producing deer and other game for sport, but were also important in the production of other vital resources such as timber and other grazing animals. The landscape parks however, were primarily for ornament and often designed as political statements in the rural landscape. They produced animals and other farm produce for the estate, but this was not the primary function. Intensive farming went on out in the 'improved' countryside beyond the park pale.

When a new, modern park took in older parkland, it gained much of its ecology. However, many parks came from former common, heath, pasture, or arable field, and these then influenced the ecology of the transformed landscape and the impacts may still be observed today. Indeed, as being shown by our current research on 'Shadow Woods', some of these landscapes included ecologies just as old and continuous as those of the medieval parks and the enclosed medieval woods. Over this modified landscape was laid out a new ecology of both planted natives but also exotic trees, shrubs and herbs from around the world; Brown was working during a 'golden age' of plant discovery and this influenced what he could achieve. Furthermore, as the eighteen century morphed into the nineteenth, as imperial Europe colonised the globe, a period of unprecedented trade and importation of exotic plants and even animals followed (see Rotherham, 2005 a, b, 2011, 2014). This process had a major impact on the evolving ecologies of Brown's landscape creations.

Certainly by the late 1700s, gardeners and landscapers were using species such as 'the wild rhododendron' (*Rhododendron ponticum*) as a major component of structure planting and design. This is rarely considered by conservationists who see the plant as a problem and garden design experts who believe it is established as an incidental and largely re-grown from rootstock used for more exotic varieties. That is simply not the case and we are very selective about what we see and how we interpret it.

Figure 7. Massed planting of oaks at Holkham Hall, Norfolk which may provide the next generation of 'veterans'

By the 1800s, William Robinson and his followers were advocating the widespread introduction of exotic herbs and shrubs into the landscape. Robinson stated that the principle of wild gardening was '*.....naturalizing or making wild innumerable beautiful natives of many regions of the earth in our woods, wild and semi-wild places, rougher parts of pleasure grounds, etc*'. Sir Joseph Hooker was soon able to observe that Himalayan balsam, a wild garden favourite, was, '*A terror to botanists, deceitful above all plants, and desperately wicked*'. However, as late as 1993, Gwynn Ellis account, described Himalayan balsam as '*Arguably one of our most attractive plants and with the added interest of exploding fruits*'. These are just a few examples of the ecological transformation that occurred in the British countryside from the 1700s onwards.

Figure 8. Rhododendron from Iberia widely planted in the landscaped parks and gardens

Beyond the park pale

Through the socio-economic and political structures and the fashions of the day, the influence of the park went beyond the pale and into the wider landscape. Associated with hunting, shooting, woodland management and the agricultural economy of the estate, there were and are significant ecological footprints.

It is suggested that whilst with 'improvement' the countryside experienced the removal of wilder landscapes beyond the pale, but with parkland enclosures, the creation of tame wilderness within the park. In the latter, it was safe for the household and even the ladies, to recreate and to play in the safety and sanctuary of a mock nature. In the sanctuary of the park, this tame wilderness had wider relationships to other movements of the eighteenth and nineteenth centuries, the Romantics and the Picturesque for example. An unnamed obituary writer suggested that '*Such, however, was the effect of his genius that when he was the happiest man, he will be least remembered; so closely did he copy nature that his works will be mistaken*'; in other words, when he had created 'wild, natural' landscapes. This was a matter of swings and roundabouts for Brown's admirers and his critics. Sir William Chambers, an authority on garden design, dismissed Brown's landscapes as differing '*....very little from common fields, so closely is nature copied in most of them*'. Not everyone liked brown's approach and when the Great Parterre at Blenheim, planted by Henry Wise, was swept away by Brown, Sir William Chambers complained. He wrote that a priceless piece of history was destroyed with whole woods swept away '*....to make room for a little grass and a few*

American weeds'. In this context, Brown's reputation quickly reduced after his death in 1783. This was in part because Brown removed many formal gardens-which people liked, and also, because the 'English Landscape style' presented a tame nature and not the dramatic conflicts and impacts of wild nature. This provoked reactions against the harmony and calmness of Brown's landscapes, which were seen as contrary to the excitements of the *'sublime'* so precious to the Romantics such as Richard Payne Knight and Uvedale Price.

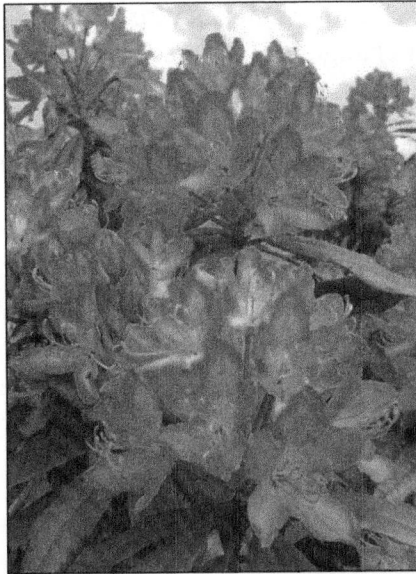

Figure 9. Close up of rhododendron – a favourite plant for landscapers and wild gardeners

Unleashing the aliens

However, it is argued too, that Brown and his associates had further and major influence on contemporary ecologies, through the introduction and fostering of exotic species. Many of these plants and animals were introduced to the British landscape by the great landscapers (e.g. Brown and Repton), or by their Victorian descendants. During his own career, Brown would have only a limited suite of exotic plants to apply to his pleasure grounds and parks. However, in order to understand Brown's ecology, and perhaps give a nod to his undoubted genius, we must recognise that he never experienced the maturity of his creations. His was a vision but not based on personal experience; he planted for future generations. In terms of ecology, Brown set in place a matrix of environmental conditions and influences, and management guidance to be followed or not by those responsible for his sites over subsequent decades and centuries. As time progressed, Brown's descendants would have increasing numbers and variety of exotic herbs, shrubs and trees to introduce to these parklands. By the Victorian period, through

Acclimatization Societies, they even released exotic fauna to embellish the vistas; some, like Reeve's muntjac are still with us today.

Brown's influence on ecology was perhaps greatest not through his direct impacts on specific sites, but his triggering of an obsession with gardens and plants through the subsequent two centuries or more. In freeing landscapes to more 'naturalistic' forms and in generating interest in the dramatic uses of exotic trees, shrubs and herbs, Brown paved the way for others to follow. Through the Wild Garden Movement and the Acclimatization Societies (see Rotherham, 2011), Brown and his successors wrought a major change in British ecology, the consequences of which still resonate across the landscape today. Over vast areas they brought about a dramatic change to recombinant or hybrid ecologies of rhododendrons, laurels, giant hogweed, Japanese knotweed, giant knotweed, Himalayan balsam and much more.

However, although visitors often view these parks as somehow 'natural' they are not. These are highly modified recombinant ecologies, which in part link to the past and resonate with the ancient but hybridised with exotics from around the world. In the recombinant ecology of the parkland today, the woods are populated by huge numbers of exotic pheasants, the lakes by vast flocks of North American Canada geese, and the open grasslands by European fallow deer.

Figure 10. Himalayan balsam – an alien unleashed by the Victorian wild gardeners

Economy & tourism

A further issue for conservation, but so far neglected, is the economic value of the Brown landscapes and the other parks and gardens. Remarkably, this is a topic almost totally neglected by the main researchers in tourism and leisure, and yet provides a powerhouse for many rural and urban-fringe economies. The landscapes and their great houses and halls function as economic growth-poles in areas that are frequently isolated with weak local economic function.

Figure 11. Chatsworth, Derbyshire and a tourism economic growth-pole for the region

In this context, we have little knowledge of the value of these parks to the UK economy, UK plc, except that it must be huge. However, we can drill deeper and ask the question for example, 'what is the value of the great and often iconic trees to the local, regional and national economies?'. Is there more we could do to maximise and grow the local and regional economic benefits? Once again, for all these questions, the answer is that we simply do not know. This may be foolhardy since in a hostile political environment as we have today, this may be the strongest political argument to support future conservation. Furthermore, attempts to gain research funding support to develop this important area have met with a significant degree of apathy; again a reflection of the silo-mentality of much UK research.

Figure 12. Lancelot 'Capability' Brown

In Conclusion

The landmark publication by Gregory *et al*. (2013), supported by the then English Heritage as part of the build-up to the Brown Tercentenary celebrations, provides a comprehensive overview of Brown, as a gardener, and a landscaper. Alongside this, there is a huge library of literature on Brown and on the other figures in the English landscape movement. However, when it comes to the ecology of Brown, a famous American pronouncement comes to mind...... '*We know the things we know, we know some of the things we don't know, but the really exciting stuff is what we don't know we don't know.... about Lancelot 'Capability' Brown*'.

In the wonderful Brownian countryside ecology, trees, history and heritage, and economy are woven into uniquely complex irreplaceable landscapes. Conservation and economy are tied together through land-use, leisure and tourism. Yet we know surprisingly little about the detailed ecology of these special places.

Finally, whilst it is clear that little is known about the detailed aspects of the ecology of Brown landscapes, there are some general observations, which seem to hold true for many sites. The veteran trees are remarkable and in combination with the wide-open grasslands and the waterbodies, hold rare species like bats. They also have remarkable faunas of rare invertebrates such as beetles and species, and floras of lichens and fungi (both associated with ancient trees but also waxcaps and others in the park grasslands). The wider landscapes of the parks, when they survive, reflect what went before with poor grassland, or ecologically richer heath, marsh, or wood. When the landscapes survive relatively intact, they are invariably managed and maintained by grazing regimes though these may differ today from what went before. Observations at Chatsworth in Derbyshire for example, suggest that waxcap fungi are indicators of the ancient medieval grasslands in early park or other grazed areas, and the parkland created from medieval arable fields lacks them. However, we need more research to confirm the value of these fungi as 'indicators' of continuity and antiquity.

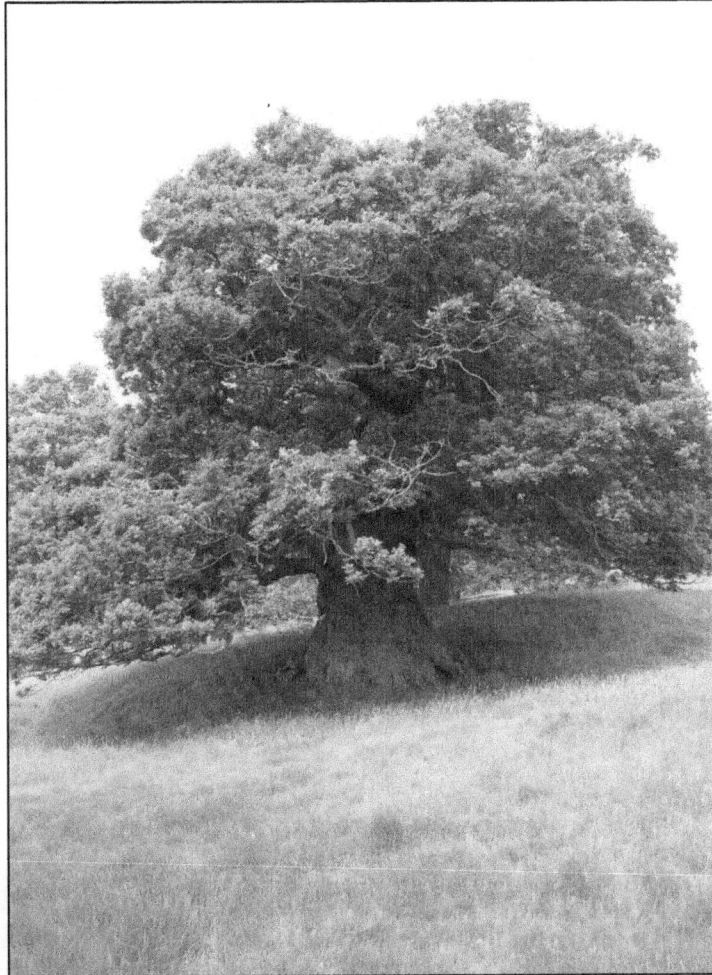

Figure 13. A great, veteran oak at Chatsworth, Derbyshire - a connection to landscapes past

Gaining a better insight in to the ecology of Brownian landscapes is a task to be considered and investigated. This is because they are obviously important and in many different ways. Furthermore, we know little of the relationships between Brown landscapes and recreation, leisure, tourism and the economic footprints today. Related to this there is a woeful absence of information on the roles of say iconic veteran trees and tourism, or of perceptions of landscape and hence on economic benefits associated with these.

Future research and conservation should seek to address these issues and the omissions. Landscape visions of future 'wilder' landscapes would also be better informed by an understanding through cross-disciplinary studies, of the roles of Brown and his associates, and of the ecologies of Brown landscapes, past, present and future. Indeed, whilst Brownian parks may be seen as designed and even manicured copies of a wild vision, they do suggest what is possible in terms of landscape-scale creation and management. Although many advocates of so-called 're-wilding' dislike the English landscape gardeners and the later Romantics, their visions and aspirations are not altogether dissimilar.

In the meantime, we also see the influence and footprint of Brown and the landscape movement in the smaller and more modest parks and gardens throughout Britain. These tame wildernesses were transformational in the landscape and in the ecology. Today, in the invasive plants, now spreading in recombinant ecologies across the countryside there is a more than a nod to the created 'wild' landscapes of the eighteenth and nineteenth centuries. In terms of conservation, there remains the question of 'when do we stop the clock?' Based on objective science and historical research we can better understand the processes and the legacy. However, the decisions of what to conserve and why, are inherently subjective, something that many carefully avoid. There may also be a lesson for the future in the ability of private entrepreneurs to transform countryside and sometimes for the better. So, what did Capability Brown do for ecology...........?

Figure 14. Clumber Park Bridge, Nottinghamshire

Bibliography

Allan, M. (1982) *William Robinson 1838 -1935: Father of the English Flower Garden*. Faber and Faber, London.

Brown, J. (1990) *Eminent Gardeners: Some people of influence and their gardens 1880 -1980*.Viking, London.

Brown, J. (1999) *The Pursuit of Paradise. A Social History of Gardens and Gardening.* Harper Collins, London.

Calthrop, D.C. (1910) *The Charm of Gardens*. Adam & Charles Black, London.

Carter, T. (1984) *The Victorian Garden*. Salem House, New Hampshire.

Clifford, J. (1974) *Capability Brown: An illustrated life of Capability Brown 1716 – 1783*. Shire Lifelines 33, Shire Publishing, Aylesbury.

Conway, H. (1996) *Public Parks*. Shire Garden History, Shire Publishing, Aylesbury.

Ellis, G.R. (1993) *Aliens in the British Flora*. National Museum of Wales, Cardiff.

Elliott, B. (1986) *Victorian Gardens*. B.T. Batsford, London.

Girling, R. (ed.) (1988) *The Making of the English Garden*. Macmillan, London

Gregory, J., Spooner, S., Williamson, T. (2013) *Lancelot 'Capability' Brown: a research impact review*. Prepared for English Heritage by the Landscape Group, University of East Anglia, English Heritage Research Report Series No. 50.

Hadfield, M. (1960) *A History of British Gardening*. Hutchinson & Co., London.

Hadfield, M. (1977) *The English Landscape Garden*. Shire Garden History, Shire Publishing, Aylesbury.

Rob, C.M. (1973) *Garden escapes and naturalized plants*. In: Green, P.S. (ed.) *Plants wild and cultivated*. E.W. Classey, Hampton, Middlesex.

Robinson, W. (1870) *The Wild Garden*. The Scolar Press, London.

Robinson, W. (1883) *The English Flower Garden and Home Grounds*. John Murray, London.

Rotherham, I.D. (2003) Alien, invasive plants in woods and forests ecology, history and perception. *Quarterly Journal of Forestry*, 97 (3), 205-212.

Rotherham, I.D. (2002) Aliens and Woodlands: impact of variegated yellow archangel. *Quarterly Journal of Forestry*, 96 (2), 128-130.

Rotherham, I.D. (2001) Rhododendron gone wild – conservation implications of *Rhododendron ponticum* in Britain. *Biologis*t, 48 (1), 7-11

Rotherham, I.D. (2003) *The ecology and history of* Rhododendron ponticum *as an invasive alien and neglected native, with impacts on fauna and flora in Britain.* In: Argent, G. & McFarlane, M. (Eds.) *Rhododendrons in horticulture and science.* Published: Royal Botanic Garden, Edinburgh. 233-246.

Rotherham, I.D. (2005) Invasive plants – ecology, history and perception. *Journal of Practical Ecology and Conservation Special Series*, No. 4, 52-62.

Rotherham, I.D. (2005) Alien Plants and the Human Touch. *Journal of Practical Ecology and Conservation Special Series*, No. 4, 63-76.

Rotherham, I.D (2007) The ecology and economics of medieval deer parks. *Landscape Archaeology and Ecology*, 6, 86-102.

Rotherham, I.D. (2007) *The Historical Ecology of Medieval Deer Parks and the Implications for Conservation.* In: Liddiard, R. (Ed.) *The Medieval Deer Park: New Perspectives*, Windgather Press, Macclesfield, 79-96.

Rotherham, I.D. (2011) *Chapter 15: History and Perception in animal and plant invasions – the case of acclimatisation and wild gardeners.* In: Rotherham, I.D. & Lambert, R. (eds.) (2011) *Invasive and Introduced Plants and Animals: Human Perceptions, Attitudes and Approaches to Management*. Earthscan, London, 233-248.

Rotherham, I.D. (2013) The ecology of Capability Brown - initial thoughts. Unpublished note for the workshop on Lancelot 'Capability' Brown – A Research Agenda for the Future, University of East Anglia, Friday 10th – Saturday 11th May 2013.

Rotherham, I.D. (2014) *Eco-history: an Introduction to Biodiversity and Conservation*. The White Horse Press, Cambridge.

Rotherham, I.D. (2016) What did Capability Brown do for ecology? *The Arb Magazine*, 172, Spring 2015, 60-62.

Sanecki, K.N. (1974) *Humphrey Repton: An illustrated life of Humphrey Repton 1752 – 1818*. Shire Lifelines 28, Shire Publishing, Aylesbury.

Taylor, C. (1983) *The Archaeology of Gardens*. Shire Archaeology, Shire Publishing, Aylesbury.

Turner, R. (1985) *Capability Brown and the eighteenth-century English landscape*. Weidenfeld & Nicolson, London.

Wilkinson, A. (2006) The Victorian Gardener. The growth of gardening & the floral world. Sutton Publishing, Stroud.

Wulf, A. & Gieben-Gamal, E. (2005) *This Other Eden: Seven Great Gardens and 300 Years of English History*. Little Brown, London.

Ian D. Rotherham is Professor of Environmental Geography and Reader in Tourism & Environmental Change in the Department of the Natural & Built Environment, Sheffield Hallam University

Continuity, Brown and the Wood Pasture Habitat: What do saproxylic beetles have to say?

Keith N.A. Alexander

Introduction

Many of our richest sites today for wood decay (saproxylic) invertebrates are actually Brown-designed landscapes, albeit those sites which also have a long and unbroken history of old trees going back into the past. While we cannot know how rich they were before the changes were initiated in the eighteenth century, or whether or not there has been an overall change in richness, it appears clear that the modification of existing historic parklands by Brown may not have been as disastrous for saproxylics as people tend to assume. This is not to say however that modern restoration or maintenance works involving Brown landscapes do not have the potential for damaging impacts on the fauna. The technology involved in carrying out landscaping works has changed over the past 250-300 years and now has considerable potential to be very damaging. Also assumptions and perceptions about how the landscapes would have appeared in Brown's time, how they were then managed, are not necessarily accurate – there is little or no documentary evidence.

Sue Clifford and Angela King (2006) in their recent book *England in Particular. A celebration of the commonplace, the local, the vernacular and the distinctive* refer to the conspiracy of nature and culture that make each place unique. And of course they are right, it is the relationships between nature and culture that make every place precious in its own way, and thereby oblige us to develop clumsy value systems in order to prioritise conservation. Their emphasis on nature and culture being interlinked is more than important, it is essential to our understanding.

Science is all too often in the habit of breaking things down into individual components, drawing conclusions in isolation, and then proving incapable of putting things back together again in good working order. This is very apparent in palaeo-ecology – by only examining botanical evidence serious mistakes in interpretation have resulted. The sub-fossil beetle fauna found in the same peat samples as the plant pollen record demonstrate a very open landscape with scattered trees – an open wood pasture structure - not the closed forest claimed by palaeo-botanists (Alexander, 2012, 2015). Science should be an integrated subject but rarely is. In contrast aesthetics is largely intangible and varies from individual to individual, changes with fashion, and is effectively impossible to analyse in a scientific way.

It is possible to combine the conservation of designed landscape gardens with wildlife conservation, through tolerance and understanding from both sides. Unfortunately, people tend to be obsessed with a particular landscape design, a particular stage in the presentation of that design, rather than the whole picture. All too often this is combined with a lack an appreciation of tree biology and tree health. The reality is that some of our richest saproxylic sites have passed through one or more phases of landscape gardening and yet still retain wildlife riches. This implies that the process of realising the capabilities of an existing site does not necessarily damage its wildlife values. However, obsessions with design rarely combine with obsessions for the reality of how the landscapers worked in the 18th century. A relaxed attitude to dead and decaying wood is apparently anathema to modern sensitivities, and yet agricultural intensification which results in poor tree health is ignored. Surely an eighteenth-century designed landscape merits an eighteenth-century approach to management rather than ill-considered adoption of everything modern technology can provide?

What types of deadwood are important?

Speaking of obsessions, it is interesting how foresters tend to obsess about volumes of dead wood. While this is to some extent a practical approach, something easy to measure, it actually seriously misses the point by focussing on an outcome (the effect) rather than the process (the cause). It is almost certainly true that the greater the volume of dead wood available at any one point in time, then the more abundant the associated fauna might be expected to be. However, the species-richness of that fauna is actually determined by other factors. One of the most important features is rarely ever taken into account in deadwood volumes – the decaying wood of living trees, especially veteran and ancient trees:

- Heartwood decay and hollowing of the trunk and main branches (Figure 1);
- Aerial dead branches, especially those shaded out beneath the living crown of the tree (Figure 2);
- Bracket fungi – not normally pathogens unless people damage the tree roots and weaken the trees.

These all have the potential to be relatively long-lived features of the trees. The other types of deadwood - which tend to be the focus of calculated deadwood volumes – are relatively short-lived:

- Standing dead trees (Figure 3);

- Fallen dead wood.

The last two are especially significant for early succession decay organisms, the cambial layer in particular being most nutritious part of a tree for decay organisms (within the first few years of death). Living wood that dies suddenly, either created by wind-blow, chain-saw activity, or rapid pathogenic activity, tends to retain all of its components from life. In the case of deadwood that results from the natural functioning of the tree, e.g. heartwood and branches in the lower crown, the tree is able to adjust the chemical composition before the tissues die, removing the more mobile substances and depositing waste products as well as other substances which slow the rate of fungal decay (Stokland *et al.*, 2012).

Figure 1. Vertical section of a veteran sweet chestnut in Petworth Park, Sussex, showing hollowed interior and accumulations of wood mould in base of cavity

Figure 2. A live mature parkland oak at Stowe showing aerial dead branches under the crown.

Figure 3. Standing dead oak, Kedleston Park, Derbyshire

Implications for the conservationist

There are more than 2,000 different species of invertebrate in Britain that are associated with the process of wood decay. These all have differing habitat requirements, different niches, and so conservation needs to be aware of the full suite of key habitats – rather than focus just on volume. Freshly dead wood in particular has a very distinctive fauna associated with the cambial layer, with early, mid and late fermentation and decomposition. Shaded-out branch-wood still attached to the tree has a different fauna to fallen branch-wood. The dead woody tissues at the centre of tree trunks are subject to a more extended period of decay and succession, one which requires considerably more time to develop. The succession from freshly dead woody tissues right through to eventual incorporation into the soil requires different timescales according to type of wood and origin. This provides phased natural slow-release fertiliser for the tree of origin, natural recycling of materials. Any removal of this material impoverishes the environment of the tree and removes resources that it might need in the future.

Conservation needs to be about process:

- The age structure of the tree population.
- The total numbers of trees, or area of habitat available.
- The density of the trees, including open-grown conditions for the development of ancient trees, as well as closer-grown trees for shadier habitat.
- Continuity of wood-decay habitats over time.

These four dimensions generate a matrix which largely explains the species-richness of places with trees. It provides both an explanation of why historic parklands are important for saproxylic fauna and a framework to guide conservation land management. On the face of it, the principles appear simple but site managers and their advisers rarely work at this level. Basically, the greater the number of trees – open-grown as well as close-grown - the more varied the age structure, the greater the variety of structure, then the greater probability of viability of the populations of the whole range of species present. These basic principles are most important on sites where these principles have been met for the longest time scale, i.e. historic wood pastures and parklands where grazing management has maintained an open canopy structure.

Clearance of fallen dead wood clearly only damages part of the fauna. Clearing standing dead trees damages a different part of the fauna. Trimming dead branches affects another group of species. Without regular survey it can be very difficult to assess impacts. The greater the level of interference the greater the damage to biodiversity. If a site is currently rich in fallen branch-wood fauna then there are two alternative explanations: regular clearance does not have a significant impact overall, or else there has been no historic precedence for clearance. Conservation needs to find a methodology for distinguishing between these two interpretations.

Moving deadwood generally results in damage, reducing the quantity of habitat available and thereby pushing species towards extinction:

- Cutting up to make it easier to transport;
- Leaving it in inappropriate situations/conditions; or
- Burning it.

Ecologically, if the reasons for its removal really are unavoidable then it should be moved:

- Sooner rather than later, to limit its colonisation by wildlife at this stage;
- As intact as possible, so that any wildlife already present is not compromised by reduced volume;
- As short a distance as acceptable, so that it does not become too isolated from its source;
- To similar situations to where it was originally found, so that for example if it was found in a well-lit situation then it may already have been colonised by species preferring those conditions and moving the wood into shade might be damaging.

Contrary to popular belief, Brown made an important contribution to the conservation of the wood pasture habitat and to wood-decay communities in Britain, especially England. By interesting the wealthier landowners in the opportunities to enhance the grounds to their mansions he contributed to the continuity of these parklands. By seeing the individual capabilities of each individual site, to some extent he merely tweaked those sites, opening up views, manipulating the ground to enhance the aesthetics. His work did not involve large-scale sweeping aside of existing trees as the majority of these were essential to the creation of instant effect, something the client could appreciate immediately. New plantings were laid out to ensure continuity of tree cover and these could potentially be thinned and adjusted as necessary. A Brown landscape design was as much an investment in the future as a current fashion statement. Continuing interest in Brown landscapes potentially helps to conserve these sites today. Meantime, in the farmland beyond, herb-rich grasslands and arable crops rich in biodiversity were steadily being destroyed in the name of agricultural improvement.

Site quality assessment for nature conservation

Site quality assessment needs to focus on species-richness rather than volumes of deadwood. A variety of options have been developed – and are being developed – in order to make site assessment more efficient and more focused. Few organisations can afford to invest in detailed species surveys, and such detailed work may merely generate data that is difficult to analyse, becoming increasingly indigestible. Sample surveys targeted at monitoring site quality and change can be much easier to apply and understand. An attractive option has been the flagship or umbrella species, where surveys focus on one or a few rare species which are relatively easy to find on demand and to identify in the field by non-specialists. Some choices have proved extremely useful in promoting wider interest and concern for wood-decay communities, eg Noble chafer *Gnorimus nobilis* (Alexander & Bower, 2011) and Violet click beetle *Limoniscus violaceus* (Alexander, 2009), and have led to considerable advances in our understanding of their conservation requirements. However, in some cases that research has demonstrated that better species might have been chosen, eg Hermit beetle *Osmoderma eremita* (not found in Britain) and Rusty click beetle *Elater ferrugineus* (fig 4), where it is now increasingly appreciated that the predator (Rusty click) has more exacting habitat requirements than the prey (the Hermit), and so the specialist predatory species within the wood decay communities are potentially the better flagship species (Ranius *et al.*, 2009).

The calculation of indices from sample surveys, however, has greater potential for site assessment as it covers the full range of species, not just particular trophic levels or particular niches. The earliest index developed for saproxylic communities in Britain was an adaptation to the Index of Ecological Continuity (IEC) – developed for use with epiphytic lichens (Rose, 1974) - which focused on identifying the richest sites for conservation designation, with an emphasis on the less mobile species adapted to old growth conditions (updated by Alexander, 2004). The concept here was accumulative survey to build up a fuller picture of the fauna present at each site. A second approach has also been developed - the Saproxylic Quality Index (SQI) - which was targeted more at assessing sites on the basis of individual site surveys and produced a relatively instant site quality assessment (Fowles *et al.*, 1999); it is especially valuable in monitoring change in site quality over time (see below).

Saproxylic site quality assessment of Brown landscape parks

If we examine the richest known historic parkland sites for saproxylic beetles (Table 1), Brown-designed landscape parks appear to be as rich as those parklands which were not modified by Brown – there is no clear evidence that Brown landscaping resulted in a decline in species-richness of this fauna. The data is not very robust however. It might be pointed out that the richest five sites do not include a Brown landscape, or that the top ten sites include just two Brown landscapes (Wimpole & Grimsthorpe), or that Brown sites feature more strongly towards the lower end of the Table. All of these comments are valid. We don't have a reliable methodology for making these comparisons.

Table 1. Historic parklands where entomological survey data is available, enabling site quality assessment for saproxylic beetles; sites landscaped by Brown in comparison with other historic parklands.

Site name	County	Brown design	IEC
Richmond Park	London		156
Bushy Park	London		153
Moccas Park	Herefs		135
Calke Park	Derbys		88
Langley Park	Bucks		87
Wimpole Park	Cambs	+	81
Duncombe Park	Yorks		77
Grimsthorpe Park	Lincs	+	74
Hatchlands Park	Surrey		72
Chirk Castle Park	Denbighs		67
Cowdray Park	Sussex		67
Knole Park	Kent		67
Kedleston Park	Derbys		65
Dunham Park	Ches		64
Croome Court Park	Worcs	+	63
Powis Castle Park	Montg		63
Clumber Park	Notts		61
Blenheim Park	Oxon	+	57
Stowe Park	Bucks		55
Croft Castle Park	Herefs		55
Wytham Park & Woods	Oxon		55
Newton Castle, Dynevor	Carms	+	54
Staverton Park	Suffolk		49
Trentham Park	Staffs		48
Petworth Park	Sussex	+	45
Donington Park	Leics		46

Wimpole Park is certainly the exceptional site amongst Brown-designed landscape parks. Values for the Index of Ecological Continuity (IEC) which reach a figure of 80 or more have been assessed as being of European significance for the conservation of saproxylic fauna (Alexander, 2004). This is supported by the presence at Wimpole of one of the largest British populations of Rusty click beetle *Elater ferrugineus* (Figure 4) as well as a substantial presence of the Red-necked click beetle *Ischnodes sanguinicollis.* Red-necked click has been assessed as being Vulnerable at a European level and Rusty click as Near Threatened (Nieto & Alexander, 2010). They are rare throughout their global range and threatened by the continuing decline in the availability of suitable hollow trees across the continent.

Figure 4. Rusty click beetle *Elater ferrugineus* (© Peter Sutton)

Pure conservation aspects

It is widely accepted that saproxylic invertebrates are under severe threat across Europe – saproxylic beetles were only the second group of insects to be assessed for a IUCN European Red List (Alexander & Nieto, 2010) and the first defined ecological species assemblage to be assessed. Rotherham (2014) equates this decline with cultural severance and this is a vitally important point, that the faunal richness is dependent on the cultural landscape to a considerable degree and yet conservation professionals are so wrapped up in their unproven hypotheses about so-called natural habitats, i.e. vegetation types, that they fail to see the reality. Amongst his examples of species declines with cultural severance in Britain, he highlights what he categorises as 'woodland invertebrates': "declines in particular species such as Stag Beetle *Lucanus cervus*, Lesser Stag Beetle *Dorcus parallelepipedus* (Figure 5) … and loss of many dead wood invertebrates from most areas." We might debate whether or not these are 'woodland' invertebrates rather than 'tree associated invertebrates' but the point is well made.

Figure 5. Lesser Stag Beetle *Dorcus parallelepipedus*

The data on extinction and decline in wood-decay invertebrates is noisy in the extreme and very difficult to dissect out in a meaningful and useful way. The important early records are infuriatingly inadequately detailed for our purposes, and result from a small number of enthusiasts relying on the travel infrastructure of the time. How can we begin to quantify the survey effort involved and make valid comparisons with the survey effort achievable today? An interesting attempt has been made for Swedish longhorn beetles (Lindhe *et al.*, 2010) but comparable data in Britain is a long way off – the Swedes are well ahead of us in so many aspects of conservation!

The use of the Saproxylic Quality Index for monitoring change in site condition
The SQI approach to site quality assessment provides a snap-shot at a particular period in time, making it a very useful tool in monitoring site condition. While series of survey datasets are not yet available for any Brown-designed landscape parks, the approach has been field-trialled for three National Trust owned historic parklands in Derbyshire (Alexander, 2014).

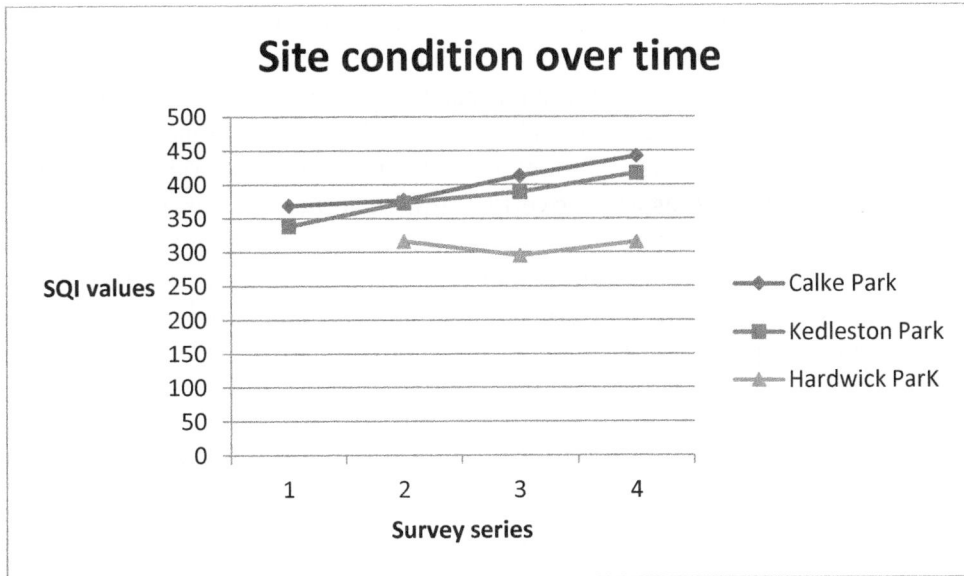

Figure 6. Analysis of changing site condition over time using the SQI

The trend-lines (Figure 6) are clearly increasing over time for both Calke and Kedleston Parks but a pattern is not clear for Hardwick Park. It would be very interesting to have comparable data for a Brown-designed landscape park.

Should we consider restoring as many aspects of the Brown landscape as possible?

Musicians today are interested to find out how music would have really sounded at the time that it was conceived and written. This involves restoring original musical instruments even to the extent of using the original sources of the component parts. String instruments with cat gut sound subtly different to those using modern strings and the products influence the way the instruments can be played as well as the sound produced. This attention to detail appears not to be so important to the conservators of landscape gardens, although why this should be so is unclear. Pasture management at the time of Brown was very different to pasture management today – the types of livestock (breed, age, sex), livestock management (grazing levels, seasonality, shepherding), and grassland management (use of fertilisers, clearance of fallen wood). So can we really be so sure that what we experience today is what would have been experienced by eighteenth century visitors? The soil and soil biodiversity of parklands today suffer very badly from cocktails of agricultural chemicals (sward applications, spray-drift from neighbouring land, drug residues in dung and urine, nitrogen deposition from the atmosphere, etc) and from compaction due to heavy stocking, use of heavy farm machinery to spray those chemicals and to top grasses when they flower and seed.

The consequences can be seen in most historical parklands as tree roots are weakened and damaged, and trees die while relatively young, often as a result of micro-organisms being favoured by their weakened condition, e.g. Acute Oak Decline, Chronic Oak Decline, etc, etc (Fay & Monck, 2016). Surely the case for a return to authentic parkland management is sufficiently strong for our conservation bodies to appreciate the issues and move forwards to authentic conservation planning? Would Brown have been thinking of landscape design in term of the use of NPK fertilisers, anthelmintics, fossil-fuel-fed heavy machinery, chain-saws? Dead wood conservation would benefit considerably from the removal of chain-saws from landscape parks. Air quality would have been much better in the 18th century too, so Brown's trees would have been much richer in epiphyte assemblages. Integrated land management should surely be the approach to conservation of historic parklands rather than trying to maintain a historic design of tree planting where those trees are sickly and die young … and where the lake is severely polluted by nutrient-enrichment and other run-offs from a sickly mode of agriculture.

Conclusions
Brown landscaping was all about nature, natural grandeur, emphasis of natural contours. He appears to have actually admired veteran trees – as evidenced from a water colour attributed to him in (Plate 36b in Stroud, 1975) – and another illustration (Plate 60b) used by Stroud (1975) shows aerial dead branches on open-grown trees at Nuneham Courtenay, Oxfordshire. He wrote:

- 'So much beauty, depending on the size of the trees …'
- '.. getting shade from the large trees …'

William Gilpin wrote enthusiastically: … [the] abundance of old timber gives the house [Cadland, Fawley, Hants], tho' lately built, so much the air and dignity of an ancient mansion that Mr Brown used to say 'It was the oldest new place he knew in England'
This was a landscaper who valued and relied upon the availability of old timber within the parklands that he was commissioned to improve. Why are these principles not part of parkland conservation today?

References
Alexander, K.N.A. (2004) Revision of the Index of Ecological Continuity as used for saproxylic beetles. *English Nature Research Report* No.**574**.

Alexander, K.N.A. (2009) The violet click beetle *Limoniscus violaceus* (Müller, PWJ) (Coleoptera, Elateridae) in England: historic landscapes, ecology and the implications for conservation action. pp.119-131, in: Buse J., Alexander K.N.A., Ranius T. & Assmann T. (eds) *Saproxylic Beetles - their role and diversity in European woodland and tree habitats.* Proceedings of the 5th Symposium and Workshop on the Conservation of Saproxylic Beetles. Sofia: Pensoft Series Faunistica No 89.

Alexander, K.N.A. (2012) What do saproxylic (wood-decay) beetles really want? Conservation should be based on practical observation rather than unstable theory. In: In Rotherham, I.D., Handley, C., Agnoletti, M. and Samojlik, T. (eds) *Trees Beyond the Wood Conference. Proceedings*, Wildtrack Publishing, Sheffield, 41-59.

Alexander, K.N.A. (2014) Saproxylic Coleoptera from Calke, Hardwick and Kedleston Parks Derbyshire: additional records including two species new to the county list and reassessment of site quality and condition. *Coleopterist* **23**: 72-77

Alexander, K.N.A. (2015) More, better and joined up - that is what saproxylic beetles have always wanted but few people have been paying attention. In: Rotherham, I. (ed) *"Wilder by Design? Managing landscape change and future ecologies*. Conference Proceedings, Wildtrack Publishing, Sheffield.

Alexander, K. & Bower, L. (2011) The Noble Chafer and Traditional Orchards - an old-growth species in the English cultural landscape. *British Wildlife* **23**: 17-22.

Clifford, S. & King, A. (2006) *England in Particular: a celebration of the commonplace, the loca, the vernacular and the distinctive*. London: Saltyard Books.

Fay, N. & Monck, G. (2016) *The Acute Oak Decline (AOD) Jigsaw Puzzle*. Notes for the Ancient Tree Forum visit to Burghley Park, March 2016.

Fowles, A.P., Alexander, K.N.A. & Key, R.S. 1999. The Saproxylic Quality Index: evaluating wooded habitats for the conservation of dead-wood Coleoptera. *Coleopterist* **8**: 121-141.

Lindhe, A., Jeppson, T. & Ehnström, B. (2010) Longhorn beetles in Sweden – changes in distribution and abundance over the last two hundred years. *Entomologisk Tidskrift* **131** (4): 241-510.
Nieto, A. & Alexander, K.N.A. (2010) *European Red List of Saproxylic Beetles*. Luxembourg: Publications Office of the European Union.

Ranius, T., Niklasson, M & Berg, N. (2009) Development of tree hollows in pedunculated oak (*Quercus robur*). *Forest Ecology & Management* **257**: 303-310.

Rose, F. (1974) The epiphytes of oak., in: Morris, M.G. & Perring, F.H. (eds) *The British Oak. Its History and Natural History*. Faringdon: Classey.

Rotherham, I.D. (2014) *Eco-history. An Introduction to Biodiversity and Conservation*. Cambridge: The White Horse Press.

Stokland, J.N., Siitonen, J. & Jonsson, B.G. (2012) *Biodiversity in Dead Wood*. Cambridge University Press.

Stroud, D. (1975) *Capability Brown*. London: Faber.

Restoring a Brownian landscape in the twenty-first century: outcomes for the historic and natural environment: a case study from Croome Park

Katherine Alker[1] and Simon Barker[2]

Garden & Park Manager, Croome Park, National Trust
[2] Wildlife & Countryside Adviser, Midlands (West), National Trust

The significance of Croome to the English landscape movement

Croome is a 730-acre (295-ha) estate in south Worcestershire owned by the National Trust. In the eighteenth century the estate was immense – over 14,000 acres (5,665 ha) – and was the seat of the 6th Earl of Coventry who inherited the place in 1751. It was the first complete landscape designed by Lancelot "Capability" Brown. It made Brown's reputation. Croome was the first landscape to be entirely designed in what was to become the essentially English style of "natural" landscape design. As the fountainhead of what became probably the greatest single English contribution to art, Croome was immensely influential. The buildings, bridges, statuary and structures which completed the design were by Brown, Adam and Wyatt, and they add further importance to the design.

Every component of the landscape at Croome is integral to the design, from Croome Court, the church, and pleasure grounds, to detailed drainage of the land and agricultural practice. The systems and techniques used for the achievement of both the aesthetic and productive aspects of the design were the most modern and most economically effective then available. Their use reflected the wider implementation of innovative investment by the 6th Earl of Coventry across the estate and the county of Worcestershire. He commissioned up and coming new talent, helping these young men establish careers and become known across the world.

The overwhelming majority of the individual components of the design, together with the effect of the whole assembled, are still intact and the National Trust has spent the past 20 years since acquisition in 1996 restoring the Grade 1 registered landscape to Brown's design and the Earl of Coventry's vision.

The impacts upon the landscape / habitats of its creation in the 18th century
Although the Snape (Figure 1)and Hopcraft plans present an accurate picture of
Brown's landscape 'as built', there are no records of the wider landscape prior to
his remodelling so one can only speculate about its appearance and the impacts of
its reconstruction. The Beighton plan of 1714 shows a formal garden set out to the
south of Croome Court, which was then a much smaller building. It is recorded that
the lake was created from Seggy Mere, so clearly it involved loss of an established
wetland, but this 'morass' (Brown memorial, erected 1790s) may have been quite
limited in extent as surviving parkland oaks within 150m of the lake clearly pre-
date the Brownian era planting (having girths of c.4.5m against girths of 3.0-3.5m
for Brownian era plantings). These trees are assumed to have been established
hedgerow trees which Brown incorporated into his designed landscape. There are
larger oaks elsewhere within the parkland, the biggest having a girth of 7.6m
(Figure 2), which must have been mature trees when Brown arrived at Croome.
Certainly, the site's outstanding interest for wood-decay invertebrates (see below),
especially associated with oaks, speaks of a long continuity of old, open grown trees
at Croome and within its surrounding landscape.

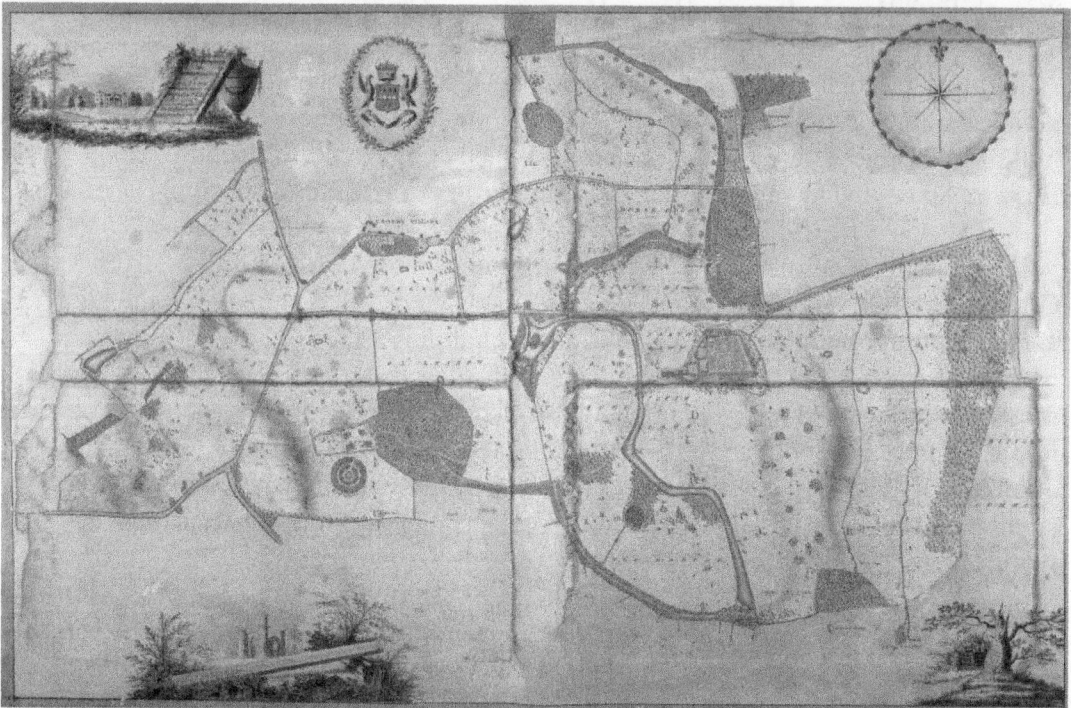

**Figure 1. Snape's 1796 plan of the Croome landscape (reproduced courtesy of the
Worcestershire Archives and Archaeological Service)**

Figure 2. The largest oak at Croome, with a gbh of 7.6m. Bredon Hill in the background

Figure 3. A tug of war contest at a RAF Defford event in the early 1940s, showing Church Hill under grassland and mature elm trees in the background

Croome in the twentieth century: post-war decline

There are no known twentieth-century records of the Croome landscape prior to the 1940s, but it is assumed that it remained predominately in pasture during the period when arable agriculture was in decline. In the Second World War part of the parkland, on the higher ground to the east, was assimilated into RAF Defford (through which it gained another significance, as the air station played a key role in the development of radar). Images from this time suggest that most of the parkland remained as grassland (Figure 3), despite the fact that elsewhere much permanent pasture was being ploughed under the influence of the 'War Ag'.

However, the second agricultural revolution which took off in the 1950s did not leave Croome unscathed. All but a few fragments of the parkland were brought into cultivation (Figure 4), with predictably damaging consequences for its mature trees and for its aquatic features, which became increasingly silted-up and nutrient-enriched. During the 1970s, the total loss of mature elm *Ulmus procera* trees, both within the parkland and across the wider landscape of the Severn and Avon Vales, compounded the impacts of agricultural intensification on the landscape and wildlife.

Whilst the open parkland was being cultivated, Brown's more formal features such as the church shrubbery, the flower garden and monuments including the Park Seat were neglected and steadily obscured by naturally regenerated scrub.

Figure 4. Harvest 2001, in front of the Temple Greenhouse

Croome's twenty-first century renaissance: restoration and adaptation

Such was the story state of the Croome landscape when it was acquired by the National Trust in 1996, with support from the Heritage Lottery Fund (to the tune of £4.9m) Royal Sun Alliance (the insurance company which had acquired much of the farmland from the former Croome estate, including the park itself) and private donors. The NT's brief was a 'full and faithful' restoration of Brown's designed landscape, but before it embarked upon this it undertook a thorough process of research, survey and planning. This was initiated before the acquisition was complete: an initial survey and assessment by the NT's in-house Biological Survey Team in 1995 (Alexander *et al.*, 1995) established that the site had significant interest for saproxylic invertebrates and this was confirmed by a more in-depth survey by the late Dr Derek Lott in 1996 (Lott, 1996). In the same year, a survey of the Croome Lake and River (Barker & Goddard, 1996) established that it supported a wide range of locally distributed plants and invertebrates plus numbers of breeding sedge warblers *Acrocephalus schoenobaenus*, reed warblers *A. scirpaceus* and reed buntings *Emberiza schoeniclus* which were significant at a county level. The common denominator between these interests was that they were associated with the 5 acres (2 ha) of swamp habitat (dominated by false bulrush *Typha latifolia* and lesser pond-sedge *Carex acutiformis*) which developed as the Croome River acted as a giant silt and nutrient trap for the intensive arable agriculture which dominated its catchment. The problem was that the Croome Lake and River was, literally and metaphorically, the central element of the designed landscape, necessitating its de-silting as a fundamental element of the restoration and thus the wholesale removal of the swamp habitat (Fuller, 2017).

The prospective loss of the emergent vegetation generated much concern amongst nature conservation interests, both within the NT and externally – understandably, Worcestershire Wildlife Trust were less than impressed by what they saw as the effective destruction of a County Wildlife Site. This concern was instrumental in the proposal to create new wetlands within the designed landscape, to mitigate the loss of the River's reedswamp. As the proposal was developed, the new wetlands were seen to have the capability of performing a second, no less important function; that of intercepting pollutants –silt and nutrients- emanating from upstream areas of the catchment before they entered the restored River.

In the event, three new wetlands, designed by Dr Nick Haycock, were constructed as part of the first major phase of landscape restoration in 2003: Lickmoor, a shallow washland created by damming the principal watercourse feeding the River from the north; Snape, pools containing both deep cores and shallow margins, intercepting a ditch carrying run-off from the adjacent M5; and Menagerie, a trapezoidal ditch channel also carrying M5 run-off, transformed into a sinuous swale marked by rushes and tussocky grasses.

The significance of the new wetlands lay not only in their functions of ecological mitigation and natural resource protection. Their intrusion within the designed parkland necessitated an acceptance by historic landscape interests that restoration of the eighteenth century landscape required adaptations to the harsh realities of a twenty-first century environment.

Development of the new wetlands
The new wetlands have proved to be dynamic habitats whose character has changed rapidly. In its early days Lickmoor was very attractive to breeding and passage wading birds –with breeding lapwing *Vanellus vanellus* and redshank *Tringa totanus*- and dabbling ducks –shelduck *Tadorna tadorna* bred successfully in 2004 and 2005, whilst winter visitors included shoveler *Anas clypeata*, wigeon *A. penelope*, gadwall *A. strepera* and pintail *A. acuta*. This attraction has declined as the development of bulky emergent vegetation has made the site less open, although the habitat which has developed is better for breeding reed bunting and sedge warbler –two of the biggest losers from the dredging of the Croome River- and flocks of teal *A. crecca* are regular in the winter.

Emergent vegetation was slower to establish in Snape wetland and received a helping hand with the planting of thousands of plugs of common reed *Phragmites australis* by volunteers in 2005. The reedbed is now well-established and supports breeding reed bunting, sedge warbler and reed warbler, albeit not in the numbers which bred in the Croome River pre-dredging. Amongst other plants within the reedswamp is the county rarity parsley water-dropwort *Oenanthe lachenalli*, successfully transplanted from the Croome River when this was dredged.

Surveys of the invertebrate fauna of the new wetlands in 2005 and 2006 (Foster, 2005, 2006) found them to be dominated by pioneer species, such as the Nationally Scarce water beetles *Berosus signaticollis* and *Hygrotus nigrolineatus*. The survey is being repeated in 2016 with initial results indicating that the pioneer water beetles have been replaced with species associated with established wetlands supporting submerged and emergent vegetation. Examples include the diving beetles *Liopterus haemorrhoidalis* and *Agabus sturmii* – the latter having established by 2007 (Foster *et al.*, 2008). Notable colonists include the Nationally Scarce whirligig beetle *Gyrinus paykulli* which lurks in flooded reed swamp around lakes, whilst non-aquatic wetland beetles with restricted distributions include the ground beetle *Demetrias imperialis*, the soldier beetle *Silis ruficollis* and the ladybird *Coccidula scutellata* (A.P. Foster pers. comm.).

Impacts of dredging

What of the Lake and River since dredging? Initially, the Lake was colonised by extensive beds of the stonewort *Chara hispida*, which is very rare in the county (Day, 2001), but this declined as more competitive submerged vegetation such as water-milfoil *Myriophyllum* sp became established. Emergent vegetation continues to be controlled by cutting or spot dredging, for landscape / presentation purposes, but sufficient survives to support vestiges of the formerly rich swamp-related invertebrate fauna (Foster *et al.*, 2008). Studies in 2016 have recorded wetland insects along the Croome River that depend on emergent wetland vegetation, including four species of reed beetle that feed either on branched bur-reed *Sparganium erectum* or bulrush - *Donacia marginata* is the most locally distributed in a national context (A.P. Foster pers. comm.).

One element of the invertebrate fauna which has expanded post-dredging is the Odonata (dragonflies and damselflies), although some of this increase is likely to be accounted for by natural range expansion. In 1996, twelve species of dragonfly and damselfly were recorded at Croome, all considered to be breeding at the site (Barker & Goddard, 1996). Following four years of transect recording by county expert Mike Averill twenty species have been recorded around the Lake alone, making Croome one of the top Worcestershire sites for Odonata (http://dragonfliesofworcestershire.weebly.com/places-to-see-dragonflies-in-worcs.html). Dragonflies have responded positively to the greatly expanded areas of open water with abundant submerged vegetation. So have less desirable species, most notably Canada goose *Branta canadensis* which is present in ever-increasing numbers and starting to have a negative effect on water quality despite control efforts.

Water quality is also compromised by continued arable cultivation within the parkland. When the National Trust bought out the farm tenancies (see below) two fields with an area of 65 acres (26 ha) were excluded, as they formed part of another tenancy and at the time funds did not permit its acquisition. Thus these fields have remained in cultivation and have drained into the Croome Lake, providing periodic inputs of silt and nutrients. Since 2012 the area of the field closest to the Lake has been taken out of production, mitigating these impacts, but some remain and the restoration of the landscape –and protection of in-field trees and ponds- will not be complete until these fields are under permanent grassland.

Arable reversion

Whilst much of the attention, not to say controversy, surrounding the restoration of the Croome landscape has focussed on the wetlands, new and old, at least as significant has been the wholesale reversion of arable to permanent grassland – 400 acres (160 ha) in total.

This process was made possible by the National Trust buying out the two main farm tenancies on the estate, a costly exercise as these were Agricultural Holdings Act (1986) tenancies which give the landlord no control over the tenant's farming activities and typically include rights of succession. Today Croome is farmed under shorter term Farm Business Tenancies which incorporate conservation clauses and the entire estate is subject to Higher Level Stewardship (HLS) agreements with Natural England, following on from the Countryside Stewardship Scheme (CSS) agreements which guided the early years of the restoration.

The reversion occurred in three phases between 2002 and 2005, most of it using a seed mix specified by the then Rural Development Service (RDS) of Defra. Using a limited palette of native grasses and wildflowers, the 'Croome mix' has proved effective at establishing a colourful and attractive sward –especially on thinner soils mown for hay- but lacks common knapweed *Centaurea nigra* and other constants of MG5 grassland, the NVC community which one would expect to occur in this situation in the absence of agricultural improvement (Rodwell, 1992).

The seed used for the initial sowings was sourced without regard for provenance, as evidenced by the rather robust nature of the bird's-foot-trefoil *Lotus corniculatus* within some of the re-established swards (although these appear no less attractive to the larvae of common blue butterflies *Polyommatus icarus* and six-spot burnet moths *Zygaena filipendulae*), but the wildflowers used in subsequent sowings were of native provenance.

Figure 5. Spreading silt, dredged from the Croome River, prior to re-seeding

Although the same seed mixture was used for most of the grassland re-establishment, 10-12 years on there is considerable variation in sward diversity between different parts of the site which reflect both the nature of the soil and subsequent management. In some areas, especially those incorporating silt dredged from the Croome River (Figure 5) and / or subject to a more intensive grazing regime, the sward is grass-dominated. However, elsewhere –most notably on Church Hill, managed by an annual hay cut and aftermath grazing- a diverse flowery sward has developed (Figure 6), with the sown plants being supplemented by natural colonisation of species including lady's bedstraw *Galium verum*, wild carrot *Daucus carota* and most recently pyramidal orchid *Anacamptis pyramidalis*.

This extensive grassland restoration has brought many benefits for the historic landscape and biodiversity, underpinned by stabilisation of soils and reduction of nutrients (no fertiliser inputs are allowed under the new tenancies). This has improved the condition of several of the seven field ponds within the site, which have value for aquatic flora and invertebrates and support amphibians including great crested newt (Watson, 2006; Dewsbury, 2011). Perhaps the primary benefit has been the reduction in the damage caused to the old parkland trees by cultivation and its associated inputs.

Figure 6. Re-established grassland, now managed as hay meadow

Croome's veteran tree: their significance for wildlife and landscape

Croome's ancient and veteran parkland trees not only provide a direct connection to the Brownian era and earlier, they also provide a range of micro-habitats which collectively support a remarkably rich assemblage of invertebrates associated with wood-decay (saproxylic species). As referenced above, a survey of Croome in 1995 (prior to acquisition of the property in 1996) by the National Trust's in-house Biological Survey Team, led by Dr Keith Alexander, established that the site had significant interest for saproxylic invertebrates associated with old parkland trees. This interest was confirmed and amplified by a specialist survey undertaken in 1996 by the late Dr Derek Lott. A repeat survey by Dr Lott in 2006 (Lott, 2007), augmented by further sampling by Andy Foster of the NT in 2007 (Foster *et al.*, 2008), recorded additional saproxylic species, such that Croome is considered to be a nationally important site according to the Index of Ecological Continuity (Alexander, 2004), with a score of 62, and the Saproxylic Quality Index (Fowles *et al.*, 1999), with a score of 623.4 (http://khepri.uk/rankings/ accessed 24/03/2016). Further sampling in 2016 has already yielded additional saproxylic species, so these scores may be expected to increase.

Some of the additional beetles are particularly significant as they depend on heart rot within veteran trees and are Red Data Book (RDB) listed: the weevil *Dryophthorus corticalis,* restricted to red rot in oak; and the click beetles *Procraerus tibialis* and *Ampedus rufipennis;* the former occurs in various tree species, whilst the latter inhabits soft white rot – often beech, but in lime at Croome. Other significant additions for Croome include species associated with decaying branches such as the RDB longhorn beetle *Grammoptera ustulata.* In addition to these RDB species at least six Nationally Notable (Scarce) wood-decay associated beetles have also been added to the recorded fauna for Croome (A.P. Foster, pers. comm.).

The richness of Croome's saproxylic communities speaks of a long continuity of old, open grown trees within the site and its surrounding landscape. Surveys of farmland beyond the NT's ownership have revealed densities of mature open grown trees comparable with parts of the parkland (unpublished data), whilst the internationally important site of Bredon Hill lies 5km to the south-east. Croome shares many species with Bredon, including the RDB longhorn beetle referenced above for which Bredon provided the only previous county record, whilst the weevil appears to be new for the Midlands area (A.P. Foster, pers. comm.).

Unfortunately much of the former Croome estate beyond the NT's boundaries remains in intensive arable, with damaging impacts on tree health. Not that conversion to grassland is a guarantee of tree protection, as stock can cause direct and indirect damage to them unless managed carefully. This has been a localised issue at Croome, for which the Trust has received justified criticism, and efforts have been made address to the problems. Particularly vulnerable trees have been fenced against stock and mulched with broadleaved woodchip, whilst parts of the parkland are now grazed by native breed cattle with early benefits to sward condition around mature trees and beyond. However, new pressures have arisen which threaten tree health.

The parkland at Croome is no stranger to threats from pests and diseases; in the 1960s and 70s many large elm trees were felled in the parkland. The elm had been a significant part of the landscape and the loss of these trees had major visual impact, in addition to loss of habitat for elm-feeding invertebrates such as the white letter hairstreak *Satyrium w-album*; albeit this butterfly clings on at the site utilising suckering re-growth of elm (pers. obs.). In recent years Acute Oak Decline has been identified in just a handful of trees at Croome, some of which have been felled and some of which have been fenced off following advice from our NT specialists and which are now showing no further signs of decline. Most recently the threat has come from *Chalara*. Apart from one ash aged over 200 years old, most of the ash on-site are young - under 25 years old. There has been positive identification of *Chalara* on a couple of the young trees and these have been removed.

These continuing pressures on trees, old and young, threaten to accentuate the 'age class crisis', where there are very few trees intermediate in age between those planted for or assimilated within Brown's design and those planted over the past 12-13 years as part of its restoration. Thousands of trees and shrubs have been planted –or, in the case of self-set but mature hawthorns *Crataegus monogyna* growing along the Croome River, successfully transplanted - faithful to the species and locations recorded in the eighteenth-century planting (with the exception of lime *Tilia* sp, used as a proxy for elm).

Unfortunately some of the early plantings had poor establishment, a symptom of the haste with which certain elements of the restoration were implemented. Six years into the ten years of HLF funding there had been an immense amount of research and planning but little action on the ground, so the main body of the restoration was compressed into a four-year period between 2002 and 2006.

Later phases of planting were undertaken to higher standards and have established well, so that there are many apparently thriving young parkland trees in evidence. Whether these will have matured in time to provide continuity of habitats for the invertebrates associated with the existing veteran trees will be for future generations to judge, but must be open to doubt.

Croome as a visitor attraction

Croome as a visitor attraction and National Trust property has been a great success; in 2003 Croome had 17,000 visitors; in 2015, there were 197,000 visitors – clearly this is a huge increase which forces us to consider visitor needs in this historic and ecological environment, and at the same time facilitating access for all across the whole property. This is greatest challenge for us at Croome and no doubt at many other National Trust places; how to welcome as many people as possible, after all our motto is 'For ever, for everyone', and balance increasing visitor numbers with the ecological needs of the species which call Croome home. One particular ecological success story is the continued presence of nightingales, in what is probably their northernmost location in the UK. They are still here, in a traditional stronghold, despite the number of visitors and the restoration work in the parkland and shelterbelts which has removed a lot of scrub, their preferred habitat. In areas which we have left untouched, and therefore which could be deemed 'unsightly' or 'messy', we can take the opportunity to inform our visitors about why it is important to leave areas like this and what sort of wildlife prefers these sorts of habitat.

The restoration of Croome to the eighteenth century design has been a positive story in many ways; the historic environment has been rebuilt, re-planted and repaired. For wildlife the situation is more complex; there have been losers as well as winners, and there is more work to be done, but on balance there have been many benefits and overall species diversity has increased. Although there is still a lot to do in terms of having the same botanical diversity that existed at Croome in the late eighteenth century, it being *'inferior only to Kew in the number, variety, and magnitude'* of plants (Young, 1801), we have produced a landscape which Brown would recognise, one which continues to grow and mature and will do for centuries to come. In conclusion there has been an overall positive and beneficial outcome for people and nature in this *c.* eighteenth century Brownian landscape renewed for the twenty-first century.

References

Alexander, K.N.A. (2004) *Revision of the Index of Ecological Continuity as used for saproxylic beetles*. English Nature Research Reports No 574. English Nature, Peterborough.

Alexander, K.N.A., Lister, J.L. & Foster, A.P. (1995) *Croome Park, Worcestershire. Biological Survey*. National Trust, Cirencester.

Barker, S.R.J. & Goddard, D.G. (1996) *Croome Park. Wetland Biological Survey*. Worcestershire Wildlife Consultancy. Unpublished report to the National Trust.

Day, J.J. (2001) *A Checklist of Worcestershire Flora*. Worcestershire Wildlife Trust, Hindlip.

Dewsbury, D. (2011) *Report of a Newt Survey of Croome Park in April 2011*. Unpublished report to the National Trust.

Foster, A.P., Barker, S.R.J. & Barker, G. (2008) *Nature Conservation Evaluation: Croome Park, Worcestershire*. National Trust, Conservation Directorate.

Foster, G. (2005) *Croome Landscape Park: Aquatic Coleoptera and other Invertebrates September 2005*. Unpublished report to the National Trust.

Foster, G. (2006) *Croome Landscape Park: Aquatic Coleoptera and other Invertebrates May 2006*. Unpublished report to the National Trust.

Fowles, A.P., Alexander, K.N.A. & Key, R.S. (1999) The Saproxylic Quality Index: evaluating wooded habitats for the conservation of dead-wood Coleoptera. *The Coleopterist*, **8**, 121-141.

Fuller, J. 2015. *The Conservation of Ornamental Lakes: Identifying and Resolving the Conflicts between Heritage and Ecological Values.* MSc. dissertation, University of Bath.

Fuller, J. (2017) Is Ecology a Barrier to the Restoration of Brown's Lakes? In: *What Capability Brown did for Ecology.* Sheffield Hallam University conference, 15 to 17 June, 2016. Sheffield. 89-116
Lott, D. (1996) *Report of beetle survey at Croome Park 1996*. Unpublished report to National Trust.

Lott, D. (2007) *Survey of dead wood invertebrates at Croome Park and Pirton, Worcestershire*. Unpublished report to National Trust.

Rodwell, J.S. (ed.), (1992) *British Plant Communities Volume 3 – Grasslands and montane communities*. Cambridge University Press, Cambridge.

Watson, W. (2006) *Croome Park Pond Survey*. Unpublished report to the National Trust.

Young, A. (1801) *Annals of Agriculture*, **37**.

Acknowledgement
The authors thank A.P. (Andy) Foster for providing interpretation of data arising from his current (as at September 2016) surveys of saproxylic and wetland invertebrates at Croome.

Capability Brown at Chatsworth: Creating a park for the Duke of Devonshire

John Barnatt

Senior Survey Archaeologist, Peak District National Park Authority

Summary

In 1759, work started on a new park at Chatsworth, designed by Capability Brown for the 4th Duke of Devonshire. Chatsworth Park is unusual in that, unlike many parks around our stately homes, it is not a modification of a long-established deer park. At Chatsworth the late medieval park lay behind the house on a steep scarp and on high land above. Apart from a slight overlap, where there are still veteran trees, Brown's park was carved out of low-lying agricultural land defined by many hedged fields to either side of the River Derwent. Persistent rumours that hills were moved for Brown are not true, for there are 'wall-to-wall' archaeological earthworks of earlier date across much of the park. The only significant earth moving comprised widening of the river in front of the house to make it 'lake-like' and the filling of old garden ponds and an ornamental 'canal' nearby.

Hedgerow trees were kept when the hedges themselves were grubbed out, with mature oaks surviving to today. Brown also planted, with a few fine beeches remaining. Several copses were retained that were perhaps designed decades before by William Kent. New features in Brown's park, as well as the wooded backdrops and 'lake', included bridges, stables and a new mill by James Paine, all carefully designed for impact. What has not been widely recognised is that there was also an outer park out of sight on Calton Pastures to the west, set aside for sporting activities.

In the nineteenth century, under the influence of Jeffry Wyatville and Joseph Paxton in particular, the Park was significantly enlarged, the park-edge village of Edensor was transformed, roads were re-routed, carriage drives and lodges built, and last but not least the park itself took on a significantly more wooded appearance compared with what Brown intended.

Key Words: Chatsworth, Chatsworth Park, Capability Brown, Dukes of Devonshire, parkland design.

Introducing Chatsworth Park

In 1759, work started in earnest on a new park at Chatsworth, designed by Capability Brown for William Cavendish, the 4th Duke of Devonshire. When completed several years later, the grand house built close to the River Derwent sat in the heart of a landscape park of great beauty, with woodlands planted on the valley sides to provide a scenic backdrop to the expanses of grass. That the Duke, who had inherited the dukedom from his father in 1755, could afford this grand scheme may well have followed from discovery of huge quantities of copper ore at his mines at Ecton in Staffordshire. What is seen today in the Park at Chatsworth incorporates earlier features and has been enlarged and altered in the nineteenth-century, in some respects therefore looking different to what Brown envisaged. The grand mid-sixteenth-century house built by William Cavendish and Elizabeth of Hardwick had been rebuilt between 1689 and 1708 in imposing classical style (Thompson, 1949; Pevsner, 1978). Formal gardens around the house, together with a large deer park on the slope above, are shown on early seventeenth-century maps and later paintings and engravings done over the next 140 years (Senior, 1617a/b; Barnatt & Williamson, 2005, Figures 10, 13, 16, 22, 33). Elements of today's landscape pre-date Brown, and features added later have also added new facets to the character of the place. Brown's transformation was but one stage, if a radical one, in a dynamic estate landscape with changes coming generation upon generation and continuing through to today.

Figure 1. Chatsworth House from Brown's park, with Stand Wood behind, and the sixteenth century hunting tower on the skyline that was once at the heart of the pre-Brown deer park

This paper derives from assessment projects commissioned by English Heritage in the 1990s, both on the archaeology of the parkland and the history of the designed landscape. A joint collaboration between Tom Williamson and the speaker brought both together, culminating in the publication of a book in 2005 (Barnatt & Williamson, 2005). Later the archaeology of the park was set in its broader Estate context (Barnatt & Bannister, 2009). This short paper provides a summary of those aspects of study that relate to Brown's park, taken from these larger works.

This paper derives from assessment projects commissioned by English Heritage in the 1990s, both on the archaeology of the parkland and the history of the designed landscape. A joint collaboration between Tom Williamson and the speaker brought both together, culminating in the publication of a book in 2005 (Barnatt & Williamson, 2005). Later the archaeology of the park was set in its broader Estate context (Barnatt & Bannister, 2009). This short paper provides a summary of those aspects of study that relate to Brown's park that is taken from these larger works.

Before Brown

Chatsworth Park is unusual in that unlike many parks around our stately homes, it is not a modification of a long-established deer park. At Chatsworth the late-medieval park lay behind the house on a steep scarp and on high land above, with The Stand, a tall hunting tower, built at the interface and visible on the skyline above the house. Apart from a slight overlap where there are still veteran oak trees, Brown's park was carved out of low-lying agricultural land defined by many hedged fields to either side of the River Derwent. In the early seventeenth-century those areas that eventually became Brown's park included fields to the east of the river to north and south of the house, and around Edensor village on the western side. On this side of the river there was also an open sheepwalk south and west of the village and an extensive open warren to the north-east (Senior, 1617a/b; Barnatt & Williamson, Figures10, 13). However, extensive earthwork evidence within the park shows that these two open areas had been fully enclosed into hedged fields by the time Brown came to Chatsworth (Barnatt & Williamson, 2005, Figures 36, 90, 92-93, 97-9). The warren, which had its fields used for pasture as well as for rearing rabbits, was closed in 1758 in advance of ripping up the boundaries when they set to work creating the park.

Well before Brown arrived in 1759, other modernisations of the eighteenth-century landscape were planned. These included schemes for removing parts of the geometrically laid out formal gardens and some of the outbuildings, kitchen gardens and roads around the house. In the gardens, the Salisbury Lawn, a large expanse of grass rising up the slope east of the house, is usually interpreted as created by Brown, but seems to be an earlier feature. It is clearly shown on a painting by Thomas Smith of Derby of *c.* 1743 (Barnatt & Williamson, Figure 41). Unless this part of the painting was overpainted after *c.* 1760, and it would be fascinating to see it x-rayed to determine if this is the case or not, then the Salisbury Lawn was already here fifteen years before Brown arrived at Chatsworth. If so, the old former seventeenth century formal gardens may have been swept away following advice from the architect and landscape designer William Kent who we know was at Chatsworth in the 1730s. A plan drawn in 1751 of features between the house and river confines itself to outbuildings, kitchen garden and parts of the formal garden (Barnatt & Williamson, Figure 43); these had all gone by about 1760 and the existence of the plan suggests their removal was being contemplated early in the 1750s; however, it is unclear whether any removals had been started for the 4th Duke before Brown arrived at Chatsworth.

Figure 2. One of the veteran oak trees in Brown's park north of the house, which until the mid-eighteenth century stood in the lower part of the old deer park

Brown at Chatsworth

While Brown was the designer of the park as a whole, it was his 'foreman' Michael Millican who oversaw much of the work done by estate labourers between 1760 and 1765. Thereafter, Millican moved to take up the post of Royal Gardner at Richmond Park, a job secured for him by Brown when the work at Chatsworth was nearly complete.

A vital part of Brown's design was the flanking woodlands on the steep slopes to either side of the valley. To the east Stand Wood, which lay within the old deer park, had long had trees but new plantings infilled areas where old woodland was sparse. To the west New Piece Plantation was a new creation and made a second strong visual statement that framed the park when viewed from the house and from the roads that passed through the parkland. Today much of the planting is coniferous and not that old, but a few surviving veteran lime trees in one sheltered area indicate Brown's planting may originally have looked very different to what we see today. What has not been widely recognised is that there was also an outer park out of sight behind New Piece Plantation on the high land of Calton Pastures, which seems to have been set aside for sporting activities. Here field boundaries only a few decades old were removed in the late 1750s, grubbed out in identical fashion to the hedges in the main park below when this was being created a year or two later.

Persistent rumours that hills were moved for Brown are not true, for there are 'wall-to-wall' archaeological earthworks of earlier date across much of the park. The only significant earth moving took place in two specific locations. The first comprised widening of the river in front of the house to make it 'lake-like', with the water held back by a high weir. The second involved the filling of old garden ponds and an ornamental 'canal' nearby; this area is one of two 'blanks' where there are no visible earlier archaeological features. Even here, adjacent to what was filled, a small area of the old formal garden layout was retained. A wooded area surrounded by parkland, known as 'The Rookery', had a small formal garden at its heart, once part of a much larger layout designed in the 16th century. This contained Queen Mary's Bower, which today is an impressive garden structure surrounded by a pond that was 'restored' by Wyatville in the 1820s. This rebuilding was done at the time the rest of the Rookery garden was removed, bringing the Bower into the parkland and leaving only low earthworks with this raised walled garden in full view. There are two other 'blanks' in the park, one where the south-eastern half of Edensor village was removed in the 1770s to 1780s and 1820s to 1830s, the other north of here over a broad area, part of which is now used as a golf course. While some earthworks remain intermittently here, much was lost when the area was ploughed during the 1939-45 war as part of the drive for arable self-sufficiency. Similarly, Calton Pasture has been ploughed in more modern times.

Within the park, hedgerow trees were kept when the hedges were grubbed out, for the most part between 1760 and 1763. Some mature oaks that started life in these hedges survive today. Brown also planted, with a few now over-mature trees such as beeches and limes remaining. When the trees within the park were assessed in the 1990s, using standard methods for measuring girths, at first glance it looked as if the mature oaks dated to the time the park was created. However, it was realised that the oldest oaks beyond the old deer park area with veteran trees, were set along the lines of relict hedge banks and thus pre-dated the park. It seems that the upland situation and the presence of sixteenth- to eighteenth-century lead smelters in the Derwent valley issuing toxic fumes had impeded tree growth and led to lesser girths than trees of similar age in many lowland situations. Several decorative copses on the west side of the river were retained by Brown that were designed decades before, perhaps by William Kent. Amongst other earlier plantings was a prominent line of four roundels on the higher land at the edge of Calton Pasture; these were absorbed into Brown's New Piece Plantation and thus lost their visual impact.

New features in Brown's park, in addition to the wooded backdrops, its scattered parkland trees and copses, and its 'lake', included re-routed roads; bridges, the stables and a mill, all designed for impact; and a new kitchen garden built away from the house. Before the park was created three main roads ran close to the house and these were all closed to create greater privacy early in 1759. In two cases, through-traffic was moved beyond the new park, while the road up the Derwent Valley was taken to the west side of the river, brought across 'One Arch Bridge' by Paine at the southern end of the park. Up-river, the old Chatsworth bridge across the Derwent was replaced by 'Three Arch Bridge', again designed by Paine. Here a new sinuous carriage drive leading to the bridge allowed fine views of the house before crossing and approaching the new main entrance to the house in the north front. This private drive was for people of the 'right sort' to approach the house. A second private drive ran northwards from the house to a point outside the park, where it met the new 1759 turnpike road from Baslow to Chesterfield; this was no doubt a convenient route for bringing goods and supplies to the house. Imposing new stables, also by Paine, were set back from the house approach at the edge of the new park. New kitchen gardens, placed behind a high wall, were created just beyond the northern edge of the park, while the medieval water mill close to the house was moved to the southern end of the new park. This building by Paine was designed in plain but aesthetically-pleasing Palladian style, made a decorative eye-catcher that displayed the refined taste of the Duke. It could be seen in the distance from the house and gardens, while the bridge bringing the new road into the park from the south, which ran closer to the mill than today's road, passed close by until this road was diverted again in the nineteenth century to a point further up the slope.

The transformation of the Chatsworth landscape was finished under the 5th Duke after the death of the old Duke in 1764. By *c.* 1770 parkland features, as noted above, including the Rookery garden, the grand stables, the 'lake' and weir, the mill and a second weir, the main road and private drives, and bridges were all in place. There was also the old warrener's lodge which was retained, three deer barns, a venison house and an ice house with adjacent ice pond. The village of Edensor lay just beyond the boundary of the park; at the bottom end of the village stood the old parsonage and the Devonshire Arms; both were removed in the late-1770s or early-1780s because they were visible from the house. The rest of Edensor was hidden behind a low ridge and was to remain for another 40 years before more extensive demolitions were to take place.

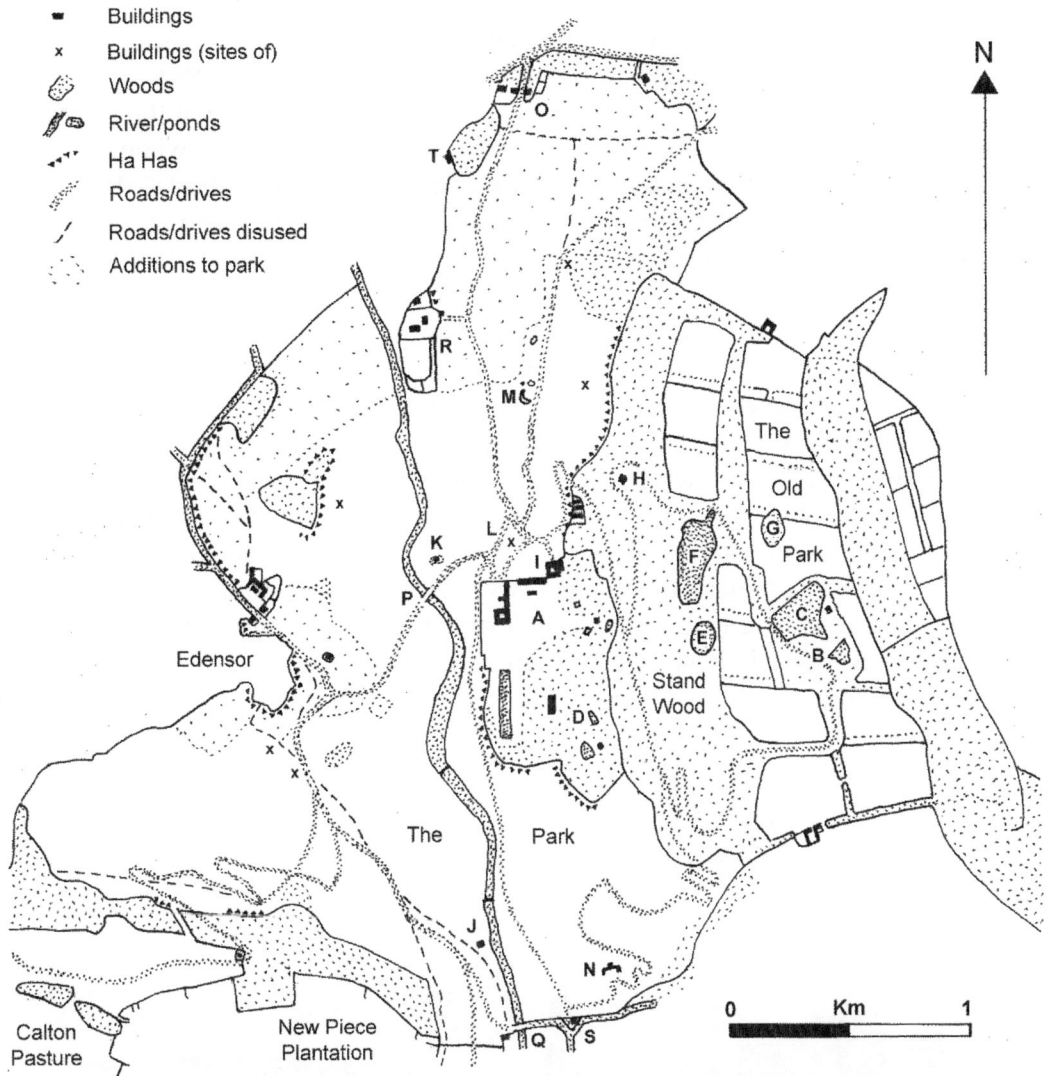

Figure 3. The Chatsworth landscape park and site of old deer park as they were in about 1900, showing Brown's eighteenth century layout together with later changes and additions (A: House and gardens, B: Old Pond, C: Swiss Lake, D: Morton Pond, E: Ring Pond, F: Emperor Lake, G: Open Pond, H: The Stand, I: The Stables, J: The Mill, K: Queen Mary's Bower, L: Game Larder, M: Ice Pond, N: Deer barn, O: The Golden Gates, P: Three Arch Bridge, Q: One Arch Bridge, R: 18th century kitchen gardens and nineteenth-century Barbrook House and White Lodge, S: Beeley Gate Lodge, T: Barbrook Lodge).

The Park in the Nineteenth Century

In the nineteenth century, after the 6th Duke succeeded in 1811 and under the influence of Jeffry Wyatville and later Joseph Paxton, two radical changes were made: the park was enlarged northwards, while later the village of Edensor was transformed to the archetypal model village we see today. The park was expanded around Edensor, where the fields immediately to north and south of the village, and others beyond the northern edge of the park west of the Derwent, were removed in the 1820s to 1830s. A more extensive enlargement on the east side of the river was made possible by an 1823 land exchange with the Duke of Rutland, when the Cavendish family acquired land in Baslow parish. Here, again in the 1820s to 1830s, the park was taken beyond the 1759 turnpike road from Baslow to Chesterfield road, with a new road built beyond to keep people out of the park.

The village of Edensor was transformed later. Demolitions here had begun in 1817 in advance of expanding the park, and these continued through the 1820s and into the 1830s. However in the mid-1830s there was a radical re-thinking, with houses in the northern half of the original village retained and re-faced and new buildings added, to make Edensor into an attractive model village. Its buildings, many in Gothic, Tudor and Italianate styles, were mostly designed by Joseph Paxton and John Robertson between 1835 and 1842. When completed, which to today's eyes seems illogical, the village was hidden from the park and from people passing on the road here by a tree screen despite having fine architect-designed houses; the trees were felled around the time the church, which now dominates the village, was added in 1867 to1870.

Figure 4. The model village of Edensor from within the park, which was remodelled in the 1830s to 1840s, with the church by Sir George Gilbert Scott added later.

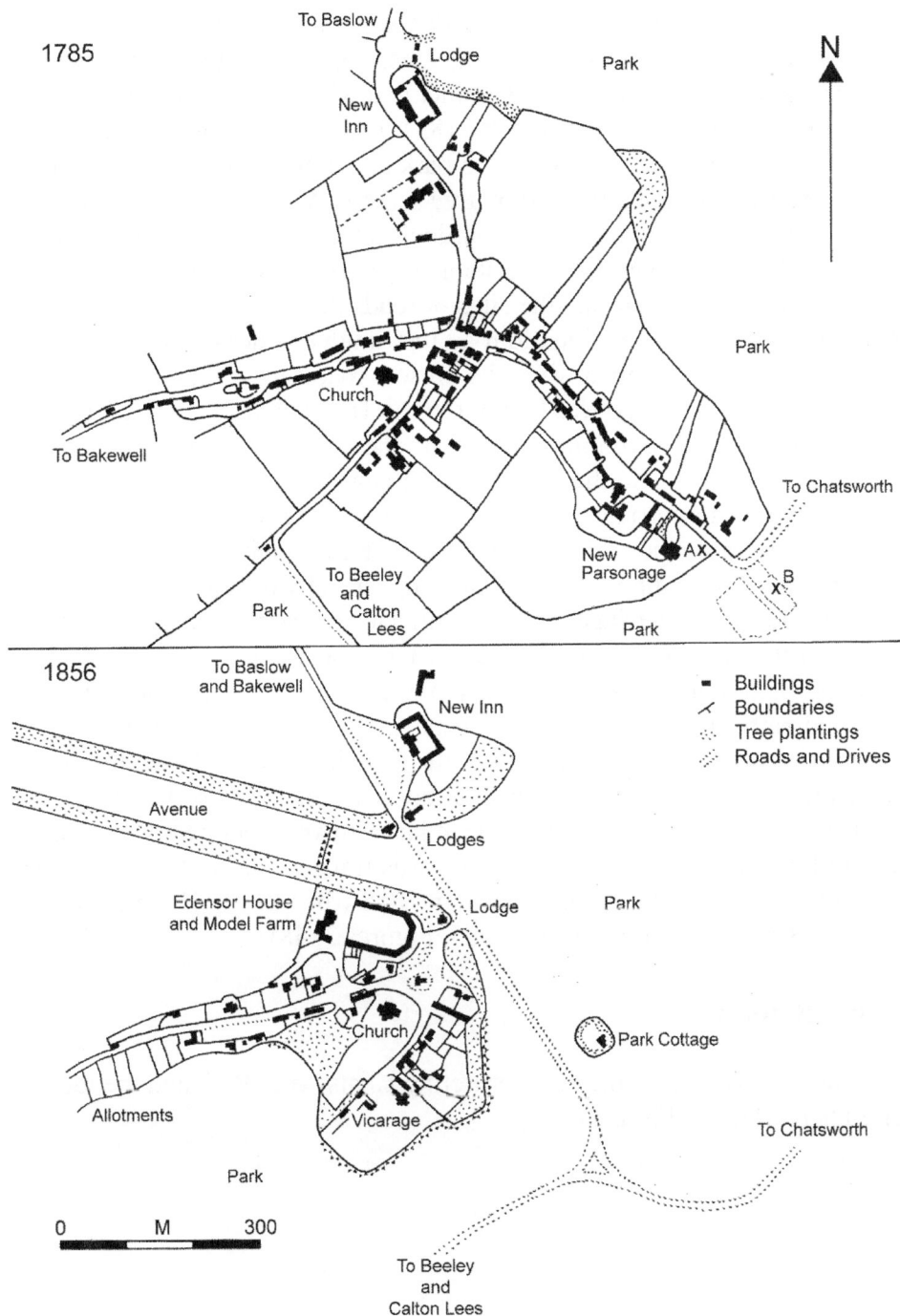

Figure 5. The village of Edensor, before and after the radical changes made in the first half of the nineteenth century, drawn from estate maps dated 1785 and 1856 (A: site of the Devonshire Arms, B: site of the Old Parsonage; both removed shortly before 1785).

There were other changes. The old deer park above the house to the east was retained into at least the 1780s, used as a large pasture that, like the landscape park below, was rented out for grazing, with summer and winter agistment agreements for livestock made every year. However, by 1831 at latest, but more probably in the 1790s, the whole of the upper part of the old park above Stand Wood had been enclosed into rectangular fields flanked by tree screens. Within this area were reservoir ponds for the waterworks in the gardens, added from the 1690s to 1840s. Returning to the landscape park below, notable amongst more minor 19th century features with earthwork remains are the sites of roads that were re-routed. For example there is a clear terrace of an old road just south of Edensor, which dates to the mid-1820s but was abandoned when the present road across the site of the southern half of Edensor village was laid out in the 1830s once houses had been cleared. Another 1820s drive running north from the house ended at the spectacular Golden Gates at the entrance to the park from the newly re-routed turnpike road. There are also two 1850s carriage drives, one on either side of the river, each rising in very sinuous fashion to the park top and beyond, built to take the Duke's visitors to see the park and surrounding scenery. They are carefully designed so that visitors seated to either side of the carriage took it in turns to see the views each time the carriage went around one of the sharp bends. After Brown's day the park also had a series of lodges built at its entrances, and a game larder was erected north of the house. Selected parts of the park boundary, especially where visible from the house or roads, acquired banks in the nineteenth century, which acted in ha-ha fashion to mask the boundary walls from view. Last but not least the park itself took on a more wooded appearance compared with what had Brown intended. An estate map drawn a short time after Brown's original park was finished shows fewer trees when compared with when Paxton left Chatsworth in 1858 when the 6th Duke died (Barker, 1773; Barnatt and Williamson, 2005, Figures 3, 48).

Acknowledgement

Tom Williamson worked with me on interpreting Chatsworth Park and the ideas summarised here as much his as mine.

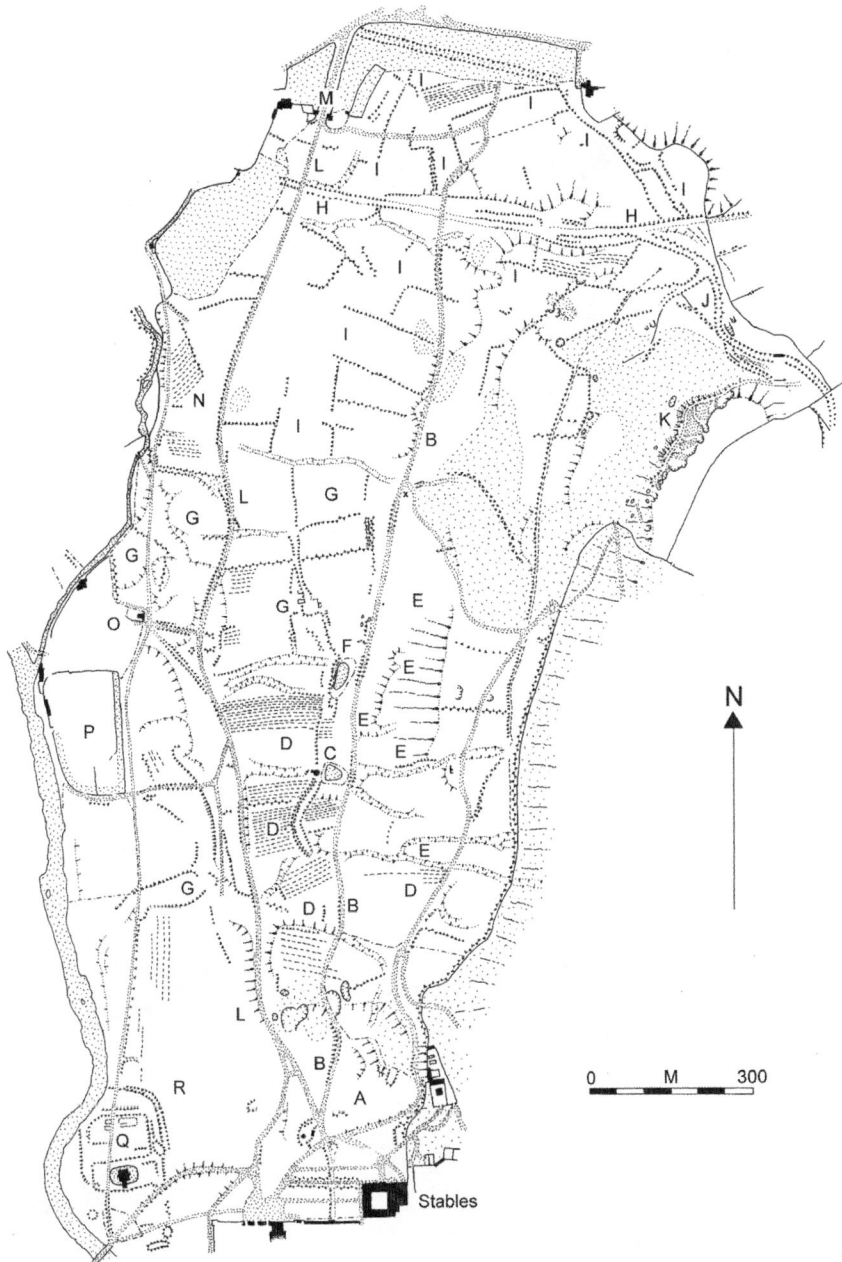

Figure 6. The north-eastern part of Chatsworth Park (A: veteran oaks, B: 1759-60s drive, C: 1759-60s ice house and pond, D: medieval ridge and furrow, E: veteran oaks, F: 1770s clay pit/pond, G: pre-park farmstead and fields in Chatsworth parish, H: 1759 Baslow to Chesterfield turnpike, I: pre-park fields in Baslow parish, J: pre-turnpike routeway, K: pre-park millstone quarries, L: 1820s drive, M: Golden Gates and Wyatville lodges, N: medieval ridge and furrow, O: White Lodge, P: 1759-60s kitchen garden, Q: Queen Mary's Bower and The Rookery garden earthworks, R: the site of filled pre-park canal and ponds).

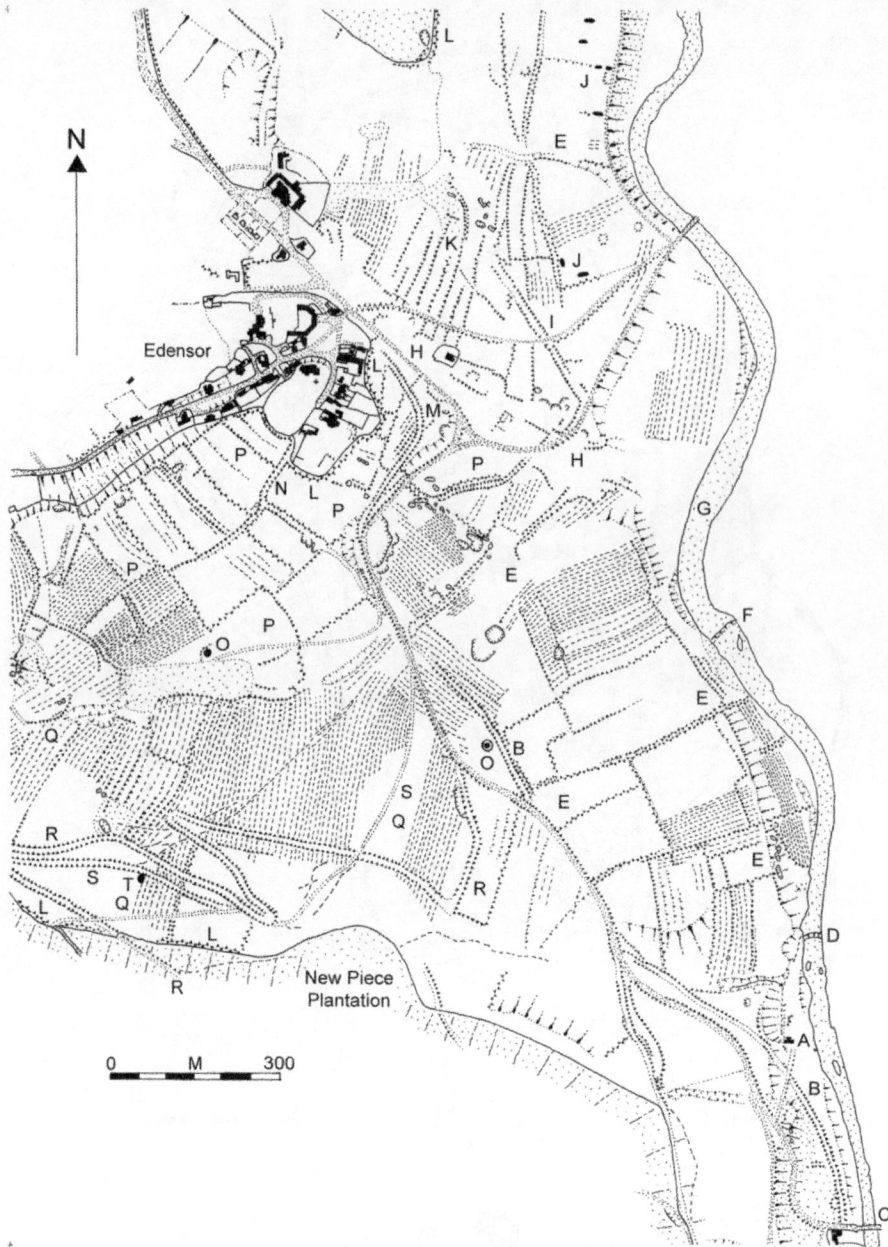

Figure 7. The south-western part of Chatsworth Park (A: 1759-60s mill, B: 1759 road, C: One Arch Bridge, D: 1838 weir on site of 1759-60s weir, E: pre-park hedge banks, F: 1759-60s weir for the 'lake', G: site of Chatsworth Bridge with mill nearby on east bank, H: Site of the demolished part of Edensor village, I: old pre-park lane, J: pre-park pillow mounds for rabbits, K: medieval strip lynchets and toft boundaries, L: ha-ha banks, M: mid-1820s road, N: pre-park Jap Lane, O: prehistoric round barrows, P: pre-park field banks with ridge and furrow, Q: medieval ridge and furrow, R: 1850s serpentine drive, S: 1820s drive, T: prehistoric round barrow).

Bibliography

Barker, G. (1773) A plan of Chatsworth Park and pleasure ground belonging to His Grace the Duke of Devonshire. Chatsworth House, map 3330.

Barnatt, J. and Williamson, T. (2005) *Chatsworth: A Landscape History.* Bollington: Windgather.

Barnatt, J. and Bannister, N. (2009) Chatsworth and Beyond: The Archaeology of a Great Estate. Bollington: Windgather.

Brailsford, S. (1751) Plan of the house and part of the gardens. Chatsworth House, uncalendared map.

Pevsner, N. (1978) *The Buildings of England: Derbyshire* (second edition). Harmondsworth: Penguin.

Senior, W. (1617a) *The mannor of Chatsworth belonging to the right honnrable William Lord Cavendish.* In: bound volume of Senior surveys, Chatsworth House.

Senior, W. (1617b) *Lees and Edensore.* In: bound volume of early seventeenth century surveys by William Senior, Chatsworth House.

Thompson, F. (1949) *A History of Chatsworth: being a supplement to the Sixth Duke of Devonshire's Handbook.* London: Country Life.

How far did 'Capability' Brown create the Rhodian Shore? Evidence from the surface waters of Oxfordshire and beyond

David Bradley

Oxfordshire Gardens Trust; Departments of Zoology and Geography, University of Oxford; and London School of Hygiene & Tropical Medicine

Introduction and hypothesis

Water loomed large in Lancelot Brown's life and work. Some of his early work was closer to being a hydraulic engineer than a landscape architect and our abiding memories of mature Brown landscapes usually have lakes or other water as dominant features. Relatively large created waters, often by damming streams, were both striking and memorable, and seem to have excited envy and imitation. To approach water from an interest in Brown is natural and has been impressively done by Steffie Shields.

This paper comes in the reverse direction: from a passion for smallish water bodies to view the historical dimension and the influence of Brown and the style he stood for, and the consequences for water of his direct and indirect influence. This is work in progress and raises more questions than it answers. It points in several directions where fascinating questions arise. What had initially seemed a rather simple calculation has in fact led us into constructing a gazetteer for Oxfordshire historic parks and gardens and to an ongoing spate of detailed mapping of small freshwater bodies in the county.

The title of Clarence Glacken's great work on the relations of nature and culture (*Traces on the Rhodian Shore*) reflects how a shipwrecked philosopher, seeing geometrical shapes drawn in the sand of the island where he was cast up, inferred human action and that the island was inhabited. But what when the actual landscape features are of human origin: the shore itself and not just the traces of human activity? Preliminary observations on the surface waters of the UK, and specifically Oxfordshire, showed that for freshwater bodies of static or slowly flowing water, above the size of farm ponds, the majority seem to have gained their existence and present form largely from what may be described as competitive landscape gardening in the eighteenth century. The direct influence of Lancelot Brown, in particular, has contributed many of the great exemplars of these freshwater bodies, much copied by the greater and lesser gentry, whose neighbours then vied with each other to make more and better lakes and pools. In short, how far did Brown's influence help to create the current freshwater habitats of England?

The specific hypothesis, that a substantial proportion of the lentic freshwaters of Oxfordshire are a consequence of competitive landscape gardening, largely in the eighteenth century, has initially been tested using two available but incomplete datasets, assembled independently of each other, on lentic freshwater bodies and on historic parks and gardens. It held up unexpectedly well, with 50% of pools in the first 200 km^2 of the Oxfordshire survey being located in parks and gardens predominantly dating back to the eighteenth century. The two databases are being used for a county-wide survey, and other counties are also being explored.

Methodology and consequences

To define the part played by historic designed water bodies of a given period in landscape requires two datasets: the numerator record of designed surface waters and a denominator of the entire surface waters of the same area. Each of these was determined by a combination of searching existing documents, maps and satellite images at various scales, often confirmed by field observation in many sites. Records of historic parks and gardens are diverse. Those sites of great design significance are registered nationally and on the Parks and Gardens website, but there are many sites with significant designed surface waters that are not nationally listed but where County Gardens Trusts have compiled more extensive lists and accumulated data to varying degrees of completeness in detail. Oxfordshire is among the areas with thorough descriptive documentation, and a rich set of relevant data sources. An early survey of historic parks and gardens was carried out by Bodfan Gruffydd in 1975-77 prior to the national lists and indeed as a precursor to the registers. It contained lists of sites, summary characteristics including the presence or absence of significant surface waters, and included relict landscapes as well as those well maintained. A much fuller list was later assembled, including large-scale maps, by Colvin and Moggridge in 1997 and is a carefully compiled record of 193 parks and gardens in all. These are all now at an advanced stage of being integrated into a more complete gazetteer being created by the Oxfordshire Gardens Trust.

For water bodies we used the totally independent inventory of standing waters compiled in relation to the European Water Directive by Hughes and colleagues in 2004 using the O.S.1983 data. Although it is in one sense now out of date (though not very, in relation to the eighteenth century) nevertheless it represents a deliberate attempt at completeness, and was completely free of deliberate historical bias in relation to the question we were addressing. It has no deliberate lower size cutoff, but the authors consider the lower limit of reliable sensitivity to be below 1 hectare. That database has 236 water bodies recorded for Oxfordshire. Each was examined at a range of scales on Ordnance Survey series 1:50,000 through to 1:2,500. Most were visited on-site, available historical sources were consulted, and each water body either classified as being substantially created or modified in the long eighteenth century in relation to the designed landscape, or definitely not so, or uncertain. Remarkably and unexpectedly (to me) over 40% of the surface waters in large parts of Oxfordshire do indeed appear to be in this category. The other major categories are reservoirs, gravel pits, other isolated pools of diverse origin, oxbow pools, and very large numbers of small ponds.

The need was felt for more detailed and recent data on the Oxfordshire water bodies, which are now being mapped with a much more thorough approach to 'limnography' (to coin a term analogous to demography for the 'pool's-eye view'), including a more exhaustive mapping of small water bodies. Because of the indefinite lower size limits of earlier work we decided to go to the 1:2,500 plan, pushing the limits towards inclusiveness. The results rather shook us, as in three 10 km squares (300 km^2) we found 677 pools as compared with the 28 in the 1983 data inventory, (a 24-fold increase); an extra 50% were added in the 1-10 hectare area and we found 507 pools under 0.1 hectares. All these were in less than 12% of the area of Oxfordshire as a whole! Laying firm foundations by making the gazetteer and getting the data on water bodies accurate has delayed the more exciting historical explorations.

The results to date will be presented and the talk will consider the ramifications raised by this work in the attempt to link limnography, nature and history and to building a basis for introducing data on biodiversity into the analysis.

Implications and an Agenda

A series of consequential research questions result as we follow this into biodiversity and the anthropology of water contact and use. Some of the implications of historical limnography for research and conservation can be summarized.

Designed surface waters of historic parks and gardens occupy an intermediate size position between large natural lakes and man-made water storage reservoirs and gravel pits on one hand, and the small ponds of farmland, villages and households on the other. To define their size, form, physical characteristics and frequency relative to other surface waters is a first step towards understanding their place in nature, culture, history and hydrology.

Because of their size, management regimes for both water and the surrounding catchment, biodiversity overall and their biologically assessed water quality, these designed historic pools may well differ from other fresh waters. As a hypothesis, do they make a special contribution to the freshwater and riparial biodiversity in the United Kingdom?

The historical hydrology of designed water bodies has not been systematically addressed, although particular examples, such as mediaeval fishponds, have been very thoroughly documented. Much information has been collected, usually as a by-product of other studies, but it has not been systematically collated from a 'waters-eye' viewpoint. This is particularly timely at the tercentenary of Lancelot Brown. He was probably more responsible than any other landscape designer for both making fashionable and constructing the surface waters of historic landscapes. What is their cultural value? That landowners were willing to spend so massively on the construction of these lakes points to their perceived value, whether it be aesthetic or symbolic. Historic parkland water bodies have an extreme range of human water contact: from almost none where they remain in private hands of highly possessive owners to very high where they are now in municipal, Cadw, National Trust, or other quasi-public or public ownership. What are the effects of these extremes upon biodiversity?

These surface waters form an unusual window into the formal aspects of habitat conservation, depending on owners, varying levels of protection of the landscape, buildings in whose gardens they lie, and of the water bodies themselves. Of interest is that their biological diversity is protected to a varying degree by legislation aimed at other purposes; they are complex examples of biological conservation but outside conservation areas in many cases.

These historic water bodies raise, and can contribute positively to, the continuing debates on the boundaries between nature and culture. Also and especially from this writer's perspective, these water bodies raise on a small scale some of the health issues of man-made lakes much discussed in relation to the tropics. Small water bodies are proportionately more important than large ones as habitats for insect vectors of disease. Moreover, global climatic change may make some of these issues more relevant to the United Kingdom in future.

Conclusion

In terms of volume of water stored, the few big reservoirs clearly predominate; along the major lowland river, the Isis/Thames, extraction of gravel has created linear clumps of flooded gravel pits. Otherwise and spread over most of the county, the role of, putatively competitive, landscape gardening, particularly from the long eighteenth century, tends to predominate for water bodies of 0.5 hectares upwards. These historic pools have some features in common, but in other respects display great diversity. While it is easy to speculate on the basis of individual cases and striking observations, there is a fascinating agenda of linking these pools to biodiversity and to human activities as a basis for informed conservation. Lancelot Brown, both directly by his own work, by his example and popularisation of an approach, and through his colleagues, imitators and successors, did most certainly extend the Rhodian Shore of lentic fresh waters in Oxfordshire, and in Britain much more widely.

Acknowledgements

Warmest thanks are due to two interns who got the gazetteer off the ground: James Harkin and Anna Cuckow; to the Oxfordshire Gardens Trust Committee for encouragement, Joanna Matthews for information on Brown's work in Oxfordshire, Will Holborow and Oxford University for supporting the interns, Tamsin Bradley and Thomas Foster for programming help, James Harkin (again) for going over endless maps in search of ponds, and the staff of Edina for constructive advice.

Brown's fragile tree legacy – whose responsibility for their future?

Jill Butler
Ancient Treescape Adviser, Woodland Trust

Introduction

There are distinct types of high value, historic tree in Brown's landscapes – the ones planted in his name and the ones that were already present which he actively wanted retained. As Capability Brown was active between 1741 and 1783 the trees planted in his landscapes would now be *c* 250 years old. For an oak this is not a great age, the tree would be in its prime. Even so they represent a huge investment in growing time and these trees are the closest to the next generation of ancient trees for which the UK is particularly remarkable. Brown, a good landscape ecologist, was ahead of his time in planting so many trees to become the ancient trees of the future.

Not all but many of Brown's designs were superimposed on previously mediaeval deer parks or wood pastures and are rich in trees that pre-date his influence. Any trees from earlier eras that he retained are even more historic and can tell us much about Brown and about his positive attitude to old and decaying trees. It is likely that these medieval treescapes had an enormous influence on him - as places like Moccas Park are still having on landscape designers today. Outside the UK, these icons of aristocratic (or nouveaux riche) power and authority have almost completely disappeared, making the British countryside unique for the number and quality of these most beautiful, biodiversity and heritage rich, treescapes. The veteran and ancient trees are the key feature – and some of these are the champions by age or size for their species in the world.

Trees as they age become increasingly vulnerable to rapid change (Fay and Butler, in press). Old trees worldwide (Lindenmayer 2016) are at risk of loss owing to their susceptibility to human influences such as intensification of agriculture, drainage, compaction and damage due to stock, vehicles or people, poor tree surgery and root severance. It is vital that we recognise the value of these historic trees, take stock of the resource and face the challenges of conserving each and every tree, partly for their stories associated with Brown and for the stories they have yet to reveal.

Figure 1. Moccas Park, rich in ancient and other veteran trees, was probably a profound influence on Capability Brown

The value of parkland trees

Owners clearly valued the beauty and diversity of their English parkland treescapes. At Felbrigg Hall in Norfolk one wrote '*day after day the verdure increases –the brilliance of the beeches, the endless diversified green of the oaks, the chestnuts richly flowering, the reluctant ashes, the hawthorns white again in spring*'. However, for them to be so 'richly flowering', they were open-grown, full-crown trees so typical of parkland and wood pasture.

They were also 'richly' beneficial for the grazing animals as the flowers gave way to large, nutritious seeds. From medieval times, the oaks, beeches and chestnuts (both sweet and horse chestnuts) were particularly valued for acorns, beech mast and chestnut production to fatten up the deer prior to the long winter. Ancient trees, especially those of light demanding species such as oak and hawthorn, cannot survive in old age as their crowns retrench and become ever smaller in height and spread. They have to be open grown all their lives or they would be outcompeted by other younger trees. Parkland or wood pasture suits their survival.

The biodiversity value of an open-crowned tree maybe many times that of a plantation tree. Research in Germany, where mature oaks have been covered completely in netting and all the leaves counted, show that there are six times as many leaves harvested from the open grown tree. Therefore one assumes six times as many flowers, pollen grains and seeds as well. Their all-round crowns and their structure of largest limbs low down on ever fattening trunks – they have a form and structure and value for biodiversity which is completely different from a commercial tree cropped perhaps at 50-100 years of age.

The biodiversity value of decaying wood was clearly recognised by Brown, and other landscape designers, as is evidenced by the drawings he incorporated in his designs and by contemporaneous painters and writers. Shortly after Brown, in 1803, Humphry Repton was writing in his book on landscape gardening '*The man of science and of taste, will discover the beauties in a tree which others would condemn for its decay.*'

Brown's Landscapes – ancient and other veteran tree richness

The Ancient Tree Inventory has been gathering data on ancient, veteran and notable trees for at least 10 years and there are over 150,000 records on the database. It is a citizen science project run in partnership between the Woodland Trust, Tree Register of the British Isles and the Ancient Tree Forum and records are still being added. The records are verified by a team of trained volunteers to ensure that the data is as robust as possible.

In 2013, the Ancient Tree Inventory data was analysed using the JNCC protocol for identification of high value assemblages of ancient and other veteran trees. The quality of sites is differentiated by the number of ancient, veteran or large diameter trees present. Many sites of value are correlated with designed landscapes on the Historic England, Register of Historic Parks and Gardens. High value sites have a minimum of 15 ancient trees, 100 veteran trees, and 15 trees with a diameter greater than 1.5m (4.71m girth). Comparison of the highest value, and therefore of internationally significant tree hotspots with Brown's designed landscapes indicates that at least twelve sites are in the high value category.

Considering that across the UK, using the data in 2013 which was and still is by no means comprehensive, there are only 62 sites of high value (red) across the UK, of which 52 are in England, the main area where Brown was active. A high proportion (6.2 %) was overlain with further tree planting by him. This has helped significantly to provide continuity of age structure at such sites. Furthermore, comparison of the location of some high value Brown treescapes shows strong correlation with medieval forests such as Sherwood Forest, Forest of Essex or Wychwood – places still very rich in ancient trees in modern times. Where there is spatial and temporal continuity between medieval treescapes and Brown, or his contemporaries' designed landscapes, this is immensely valuable for biodiversity of old trees – primarily decaying wood and mycorrhizal fungi, decaying wood invertebrates and lichens. The older pre-Brown trees in these landscapes become even more valuable as habitat and should be considered as key features in the management of the sites.

Figure 2. Hotspots of ancient and other veteran trees which are also Brown designed landscapes

A recent research project (Farjon, in press) has focused on the ancient oaks of England. At completion of the research Aljos Farjon had identified 115 maiden and pollard oaks over 9m in girth largely located using the Ancient Tree Inventory. Comparison was also made with all other known records from countries in Europe including Scotland, Wales and Northern Ireland where there are 97 oaks of this girth or more. This makes England especially rich in ancient oaks, a priority for conservation and many are in Brown landscapes. One of the top Brown sites is Blenheim Park where there are four such medieval trees including one over 10m in girth which could be over 1,000 years old.

Such important historic trees and landscapes deserve national and international recognition to raise their status and show value. The Woodland Trust in partnership with the Ancient Tree Forum has campaigned for **V.I Tree** status for trees of national special interest with the primary aim of generating help for owners (like local authorities and private landowners) to facilitate access to specialist advice and grants, so trees can be cared for as they become even older and grander with age.

Advice for owners

Interest in ancient and other veteran trees and their management is relatively recent. In 2000, the first ancient or veteran tree handbook (Read, 2000) was published and followed by another (Lonsdale, 2013) just over a decade later. There are a number of Ancient Tree Guides produced by the Woodland Trust and Ancient Tree Forum on farming, historic landscapes, events and tree establishment which provide further guidance.

In Brown landscapes there are a number of potential threats to the longevity of the historic trees and associated habitat:

- Increased public access resulting in the direct loss of trees due to the construction of new facilities e.g. extensions of parking areas, or indirect damage to tree roots from increased footfall.
- Crown pruning due to the increased risk posed by large, aging trees and visitors.
- Root and trunk damage from intensification of agriculture both cultivation, use of chemicals and over stocking.
- Removal of dead or dying trees and fallen wood.
- Removal of flowering scrub

The seriousness of these impacts are often not perceived or understood by owners or their advisors and so action is not taken to prevent them. In some instances there are major difficulties due to long term farm tenancy agreements.

Who then will champion the high value trees in Brown landscapes? Every person and stakeholder should be raising awareness of the significance of the historic and wildlife rich trees. Trees are marvellous organisms, they are good citizens – giving their all, day after day, season after season and ask for no thanks. Surely they deserve a better return from us? More people are needed to survey and record historic and other trees of special interest, to advise on the care of the existing trees and there is a need to create much bigger areas of parkland to buffer and extend existing hot spots. We need many more modern-day Browns.

Figure 3. The damage to this ancient oak in designed parkland should be identified and prevented

References

Ancient Tree Inventory *www.ancienttreehunt.org.uk*

Ancient Tree Guides 1-8. Woodland Trust.

Fay, N. & Butler, J. (2017) *Management and Conservation of ancient and other veteran trees.* In Urban Forestry. Chapter 34. Routledge, London.

Farjon, A., (in press) *Ancient oaks in the English Landscape*. Kew, London.

Lindenmayer, D. & Laurance, W.F. (2016) The ecology, distribution, conservation and management of large old trees. *Biological Reviews* 000-000 DOI: 10.1111/brv.12290 Cambridge Philosophical Society

Lonsdale, D. (ed.) (2013) *Ancient and other veteran trees: further guidance on management*. The Tree Council.

Read, H. (ed.) (2000) *Veteran trees a guide to good management*. English Nature.

Repton, H. (2003) *Observations on the Theory and Practice of Landscape Gardening*. Facsimile Publisher, India.

Portraying 'Capability' Brown's Yorkshire Landscapes: The Georgian country house portrait as an art of public relations

Patrick Eyres
Wentworth Castle Gardens Heritage Trust / The New Arcadian Journal

The words frequently used to describe the landscapes of the celebrity designer, Lancelot 'Capability' Brown (1716-1783) – such as 'natural', 'pastoral', 'Arcadian', and 'picturesque' – can equally be applied to the imagery of these places created by Georgian artists. Even though it might seem paradoxical, these words aestheticise landscapes that were utterly modern, and both the places and their representations promoted each landowner as they wished to be seen – as fashionably progressive. The genre of art known as the country house portrait was an exercise in public relations, and it was common practice for paintings to be reproduced as monochrome prints for individual distribution and also for publication in books. Thus it was acceptable for artistic licence to take liberties with topographical accuracy because the point of these images was to promote the landowner as an epitome of the culture of improvement. As a creative entrepreneur, water engineer and landscape architect, Brown was a prominent exponent of this culture, and to commission the place-maker was itself a statement of the patron's modernity. Improvement was the watchword of the Agricultural Revolution. The term signified modernity through the union of commercial profit and cultural display on the country estates of those aristocrats who invested in new farming practices. These landowners took pride in the increasing yield of cattle, crops and timber on an estate aestheticised by the landscaping of mansion, park, gardens and monuments. However, the artist's task was not to suggest the source of invested wealth. It must be said that, since the bicentenary of the abolition of the slave trade in 2007, the relationship between the country estate and the Atlantic slave economy has come under scrutiny.

Numerous artists produced oil and watercolour paintings of 'Capability' Brown's Yorkshire landscapes, for example: Thomas Bardwell, George Cuit, George Barrett, Paul Sandby, Francis Nicholson, Michael Angelo Rooker, Thomas Girtin and J.M.W. Turner, to name but a few. Nevertheless, for the purposes of this paper, I shall focus on monochrome images created for print. But first, a word of warning. Although these images can be informative about topographical developments, they can also be misleading. Temple Newsam is a case in point. Brown was commissioned by Charles Ingram, ninth Viscount Irwin for the improvements undertaken between 1762 and 1770. Lady Irwin had envisaged Brown's design as an evocation of the painting by

Claude Lorrain that hung in the mansion. Lorrain's paintings were renowned as pastoral representations of the Roman Campagna, and this canvas (c.1638) displayed the characteristic synthesis of water, woods and ruinous classical temples. A similarly Italianate ambiance suffused the painting by Michael Angelo Rooker, *A Prospect of Temple Newsam, c.*1765, which was commissioned in response to Brown's appreciation of the capabilities of the place. Although the artist emphasised the lake as a spectacular feature, it was never realised. Yet, over twenty years later, James Lambert's *Temple Newsam from the East* (Figure 1), depicts the same watery spectacle. By 1786, further improvements were underway around the mansion and Lambert's painting serves both as a reminder of the original intention and as a suggestion that the lake was still under consideration. Thus these two paintings stand as records of intent, anticipation and possibility. Indeed, they function in the same way as a modern 'artist's impression' of a proposed or ongoing development, which may bear little relation to the completed project.

Figure 1. James Lambert, *Temple Newsam from the East*, wash drawing, 1786 (© Leeds Museums and Galleries), reproduced in *Yorkshire Capabilities*: *New Arcadian Journal 75/76*, 2016

Temple Newsam is among the twenty-three Yorkshire landscapes attributed to Brown by Karen Lynch in the book *Yorkshire Capabilities*.[i] Significantly, she has established that fourteen of these are securely documented through archive records. The other nine are either unconnected with Brown or Brownian. The term 'Brownian' is generally used to describe Georgian landscapes that bear the familiar hallmarks of the place-maker even though they may have been designed by one of the numerous professionals of the landscape movement or even by the landowner. Wentworth Castle is among the latter and the likelihood of the park being designed by Brown is based on the assertions of two authors: George Mason in 1768 and 1795, and Joseph Wilkinson in 1883.[ii]

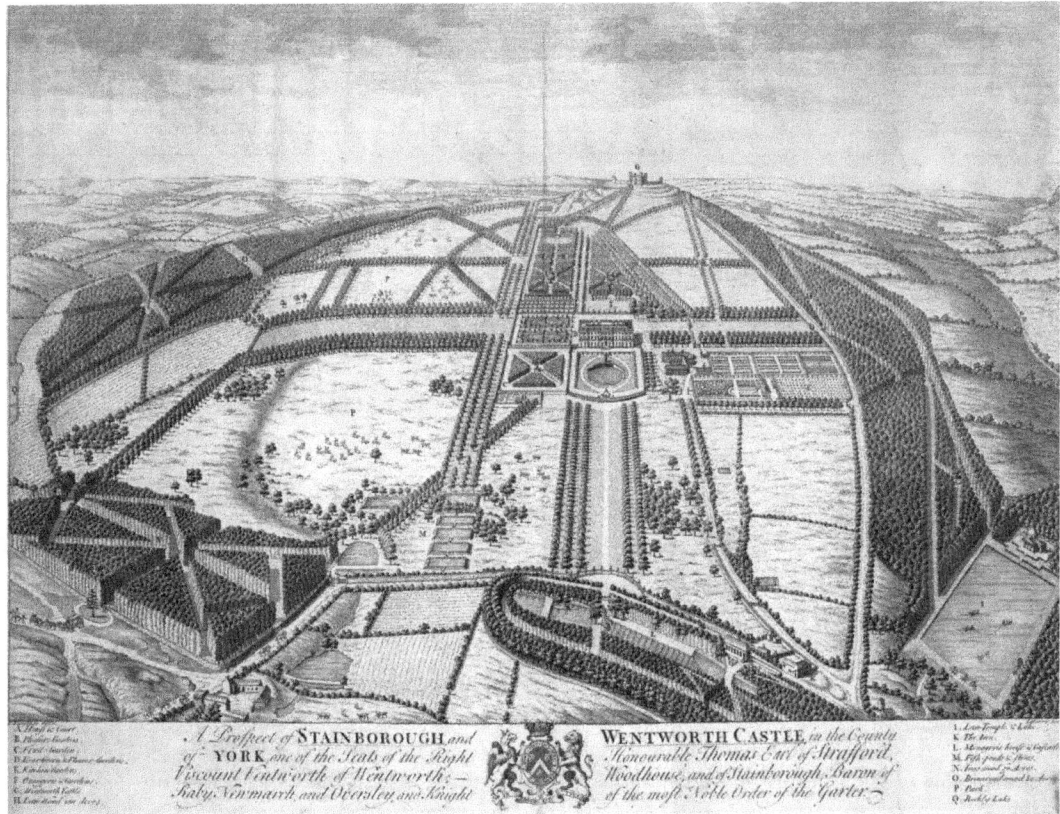

Figure 2. John Harris after Thomas Badeslade, *View of Stainborough and Wentworth Castle*, engraving, 1730, published in *Vitruvius Brittanicus* [sic], 1739, and *Britannia Illustrata*, 1740 (© British Library)

Two prints portray Wentworth Castle before and after the era of Brown. Thomas Badeslade's overview of 1730 (Figure 2) is representative of the tradition of topographical bird's-eye views popularised by Leonard Knyff and the engraver Jan Kip, who had produced the two earlier views of Wentworth Castle in 1711 and 1714. Badeslade depicts the modernity of a must-have Baroque landscape whose sylvan geometry in park and gardens alike records the influence of French and Dutch design – and combines the visible with the anticipated. Almost a century later, Jonathan Neale's view of 1822 (Figure 3) depicts the place transformed by the naturalistic style advocated by the English landscape movement and its most illustrious designer, 'Capability' Brown. A river is shown flowing through the park, whose greensward is grazed by cattle and deer and sweeps up to the front door in Brownian style, while the mansion itself is embowered within profuse woodland wherein a temple can be glimpsed. As such, Neale's view is evocative of the landscapes painted by Thomas Bardwell in the early

1750s. Bardwell's paintings also indicate that 'Capability' Brown was not the place-maker at Wentworth Castle.

Figure 3. C. Askey after Jonathan Neale, *Wentworth Castle across the Serpentine River*, engraving for Neale's *Views of the Seats of Noblemen and Gentlemen*, vol. 5, 1822 (© Leeds Library and Information Service), reproduced in *Yorkshire Capabilities*: *New Arcadian Journal 75/76*, 2016

Although the estate archives record payment for these paintings, they have not yet yielded up evidence of Brown working at Wentworth Castle. However, at the time of Bardwell's paintings, 'Capability' was only just embarking on his career as an independent landscape designer in the south of England, and did not begin to work in Yorkshire until 1758.[iii] Moreover the estate archives have surprisingly revealed that the sinuous, canalised and Brown-like waterway, known as the Serpentine River, had already been completed in 1738 by the first Earl of Strafford (second creation).[iv] His son the second Earl later extended it during 1749-1758 and again in 1773.[v] Attribution to Brown is further compromised by Horace Walpole, fourth Earl of Orford. Walpole was among the authors who knew, admired and promoted the place-maker as the apogee of the landscape movement. Nonetheless in his influential *History of the Modern Taste in Gardening*, 1771 and 1780, Walpole identified the second Earl as the designer of the Brownian parkland as well as the new Palladian wing of the mansion.[vi] Bardwell's two paintings (1751-1752) are consummate examples of artistic public relations. In portraying the park as a Brownian model of the English landscape style, Bardwell presented the landowner as a man of modern taste and as an aristocratic exponent of landscape gardening and agricultural improvement. He also created a record of what the second Earl had already achieved combined with the anticipated improvements that would take a further twenty years to complete.

Further to the north, Harewood is an exemplar of the way that improvement through investment of commercial wealth in land, agriculture and conspicuous display ensured the elevation of a gentry merchant family into the aristocracy. This makeover took place in phases between 1759 and 1790 as Edwin Lascelles hired the succession of professional designers to implement the fashionable requirements of improvement.[vii] The Palladian villa was designed by John Carr, the interiors by Robert Adam and the furniture and furnishings by Thomas Chippendale. Between 1772 and 1781, 'Capability' Brown created the lake and also landscaped the park,[viii] after which pleasure grounds and garden buildings were constructed. In 1790, Edwin Lascelles was ennobled as first Baron Harewood and in 1812 his successor, Edward Lascelles, was further elevated from second Baron to first Earl of Harewood.

Figure 4. C. Askey after Jonathan Neale, *Harewood House*, engraving for Neale's *Views of the Seats of Noblemen and Gentlemen*, vol. 5, 1822 (© Leeds Library and Information Service), reproduced in *Yorkshire Capabilities*: *New Arcadian Journal 75/76*, 2016

During the 1790s, J.M.W. Turner was among the artists commissioned to paint the watercolours that were displayed in the mansion's public rooms.[ix] The task of the artists was to portray the brand new Harewood House presiding over Brown's watered and timbered parkland whose greenswards were grazed by flocks of cattle, deer and sheep. This idyll was portrayed in 1822 by Jonathan Neale (Figure 4). Turner however injected a romantic charge into all his watercolours of Harewood through the inclusion of specific detail and patriotic symbolism. Whereas Neale's landscape is unpeopled, apart from those inferred by the leisurely sailing boat, Turner included the agricultural labourers who serviced this Arcadia – as can be seen in his *Harewood House*, which was painted in 1798 and later engraved for publication (Figure 5). Furthermore young oak trees populate each foreground.

Figure 5. J. Scott after J.M.W. Turner, *Harewood House*, engraving for T.D. Whitaker's *Leodis and Elmete*, 1816 (© The Leeds Library), reproduced in *Yorkshire Capabilities*: *New Arcadian Journal 75/76*, 2016

Oak trees abound in Turner's topographical watercolours. During and after the Great War with France (1793-1815), Turner's oaks drew on iconographies popularised during Brown's career. Edmund Burke's speech in Parliament condemning the French Revolution had celebrated Britain's aristocracy as the oaks that supported the constitution, thus re-invigorating the tree as a symbol of a patriotic and progressive nobility. Turner's emphasis on young oaks acknowledged the status of the Lascelles as recently elevated aristocrats. Moreover, Turner had painted the watercolour in the wake of the tumultuous news that Admiral Nelson had annihilated the French fleet at the Battle of the Nile on 1st August 1798. For Turner, his patrons and their audiences, the symbol of the oak was resonant with a constellation of familiar associations. These encompassed the aristocracy as the bulwark of the constitution, the recent elevation of this particular noble dynasty, the wooden walls of the warships of the British navy, the hearts of oak of British sailors and the patriotism of timber production on country estates – all of which coalesced into the perception that the landowning aristocracy ensured Britain's constitutional and naval supremacy over the French republican foe.[x]

The patriotic naval symbolism of the oak had been re-established during the Seven Years War, while Brown's career as an independent consultant was beginning to flourish. Previously the oak had been appropriated by the exiled and Catholic Stuart monarchy and their Jacobite supporters. It was after the Stuart cause had been finally defeated at Culloden in 1746, that the oak began to be retrieved as Protestant and patriotic. The defining moment came in 1759 during the *Annus Mirabilis*, year of victories worldwide, which was concluded by the naval victory in Quiberon Bay. To commemorate the navy's defeat of a planned French invasion, the playwright and impresario David Garrick penned *Heart of Oak* and, with the score composed by Thomas Arne, it was first performed that year as part of Garrick's pantomime *Harlequin's Invasion* at the Theatre Royal, Drury Lane. The first verse and chorus are as follows:

> Come cheer up my lads, 'tis to glory we steer,
> To add something new to this glorious year;
> To honour we call you, not press you like slaves,
> For who are so free as the sons of the waves?
>
> Heart of oak are our ships, jolly tars are our men,
> We always are ready; Steady, boys, steady!
> We'll fight and we'll conquer again and again.

Garrick and Brown were friends and the place-maker was consulted about the playwright's garden beside the Thames at Hampton House. It was in his play, *Lethe*, that Garrick popularised the nickname 'Capability'.

It was also during the Seven Years War that the Society for the Promotion of Arts, Manufactures and Commerce (now the R.S.A.) struck a gold medal that was awarded annually for the landowner who planted the largest number of oaks – and Brown became renowned for planting oaks on behalf of his patrons, and also for highlighting veteran oaks as eye-catchers. Indeed, the only monument dedicated to Brown in his lifetime was erected at Wrest Park, Bedfordshire, in 1760 during the same war. It is appropriately topped, not with a statue or an urn, but with an acorn. Moreover Brown was a friend, admirer and client of the wartime prime minister and strategist of victory, William Pitt the Elder. An anecdote, doubtless apocryphal, is told of their farewells after a chance meeting. Pitt bids Brown "Go you and adorn England", to which 'Capability' replied "Go you and save it".[xi] Turner's inclusion of young oaks in his watercolours of 'Capability's' Harewood exemplifies the patriotic continuity of the oaken symbolism proclaimed by Garrick's lyrics and Brown's landscaping.

While Harewood offers a splendid example of upward mobility and dynastic projection through the culture of improvement, it also exemplifies the way this process was financed through the adroit cultural laundering of wealth derived from the Atlantic slave economy.[xii] When English Heritage published *Slavery and the British Country House* in 2013, the editors proposed, rather cautiously, that "the erection, renovation and occupation of a significant number of Britain's stately homes between the 1660s and 1820s" was funded by wealth accrued through trade in and the labour of enslaved Africans.[xiii] They also considered that there were wider, more indirect slavery associations with these properties. Some of these are discussed in *The Blackamoor & The Georgian Garden*, such as investment in shipping and produce as well as in companies engaged in the trading, financing and servicing of the Atlantic slave economy. The income generated by these investments appealed to all levels of polite society from the middle classes to the gentry, aristocracy and the monarch.[xiv] Dresser and Hann also make the point that the country-house-building merchants and landed elite increasingly used "notions of gentility, sensibility and cultural refinement in part to distance themselves from their actual connection to the Atlantic slave economy".[xv] The Lascelles of Harewood House were among those who invested slave trade wealth in land and conspicuous display in order to gain entry into the elite. Once aristocrats, they consolidated their status by further investing this wealth in estate improvement.

During 1998-1999 the Harewood House Trust commendably initiated and sponsored a study by the University of York of the Lascelles' involvement in Caribbean trade and slavery. The result was the publication in 2006 of Simon Smith's *Slavery, Family, and Gentry Capitalism in the British Atlantic: The World of the Lascelles, 1648-1834*. The unprecedented detail of business and investment practices exemplifies the ways in which British merchants and the landed elite were involved in and benefited from the Atlantic slave economy.[xvi] By the time of his death in 1753, the Yorkshire gentry merchant, Henry Lascelles, had amassed a fortune that has been estimated to be in the region of £500,000 – approximately £48 million today – which meant that he was among the richest of Britons. It was this wealth and the continuing income from the slave economy that culturally embellished Harewood. Yet Britain's Atlantic world remained invisible in Turner's watercolours, which provide exquisite portraits of 'Capability' Brown's quintessentially English and work-a-day aristocratic landscape. However modern Harewood is to be congratulated for initiating scrutiny of the estate's participation in the Atlantic slave economy.[xvii] This is all the more commendable given the reluctance to acknowledge this history that appears to pervade the world of Britain's country house heritage.

Figure 6. J. Scott after J.M.W. Turner, Aske Hall, engraving for T.D. Whitaker's *History of Richmondshire*, 1823 (© The Leeds Library), reproduced in *Yorkshire Capabilities*: *New Arcadian Journal 75/76*, 2016

Harewood is doubtless symptomatic of the way that improvement was funded elsewhere, and there must have been many of Brown's commissions that benefited from wealth made directly or indirectly through the slave economy.[xviii] Aske Hall is another in Yorkshire and other examples across the country can be found on the website of the University College London project, *Legacies of British Slave-ownership*.[xix] Sir Lawrence Dundas had made his fortune as a military contractor during the War of Austrian Succession and the Seven Years War, and by the mid-1760s he had acquired two Caribbean sugar plantations, one in Domenica and the other in Grenada. By 1769, he had invested in the slave-trading East India Company to the value of £192,000 and in the same year he consulted Brown about the capabilities of Aske.[xx] Just as at Harewood, the Atlantic world is invisible in Turner's watercolour of Aske Hall (Fig. 6). However in *Yorkshire Capabilities* artists have engaged with the challenge of rendering visible the links between the Atlantic slave economy and the Georgian country estate. Through her collage, *Castle Bruce, Domenica* (Figure 7), Carol Sorhaindo has combined documentary material from the Aske Hall estate in the North Yorkshire County Archives with fragments of the derelict sugar mill and the plants that thrive on the ruined building. The double page spread from the *Castle Bruce monthly Journal for*

September 1777 lists the total numbers of enslaved Africans by gender and age alongside the quantities of rum they produced.

Cannon Hall is among the Yorkshire gentry estates formerly associated with 'Capability' Brown. The Spencer family's archive has revealed the evidence of the "adventure in the slave trade" discussed by Michael Charlesworth in *The Blackamoor & The Georgian Garden*.[xxi] In his accompanying illustration (Figure 8), Chris Broughton presents the landscape garden as the rolling Atlantic in which distant trees and foreground boughs become the surf of breaking waves. He positions the hitherto invisible yet purpose-built slave ship named the 'Cannon Hall' alongside the eponymous mansion and within the swell of the Brownian park.

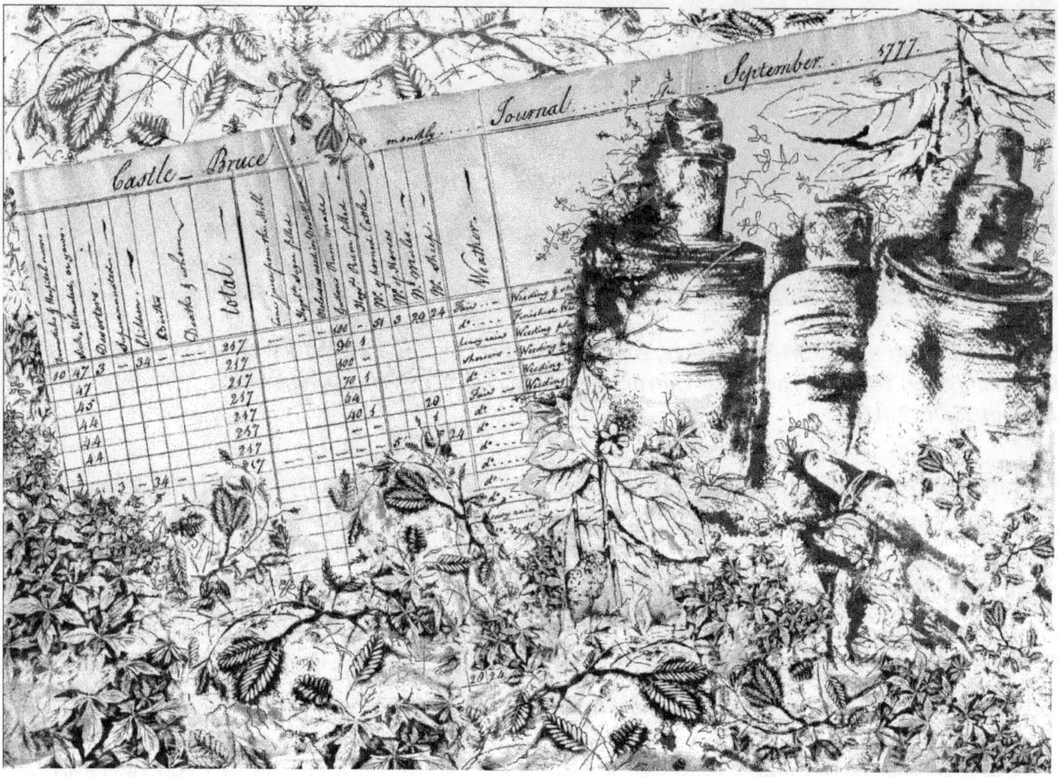

Figure 7. Carol Sorhaindo, *Castle Bruce, Domenica*, collage and drawing for *Yorkshire Capabilities: New Arcadian Journal 75/76*, 2016 (© the artist and the New Arcadian Press)

Figure 8. Chris Broughton, *Cannon Hall*, drawing for *The Blackamoor & The Georgian Garden: New Arcadian Journal 69/70*, 2011 (© the artist and the New Arcadian Press)

The evidence that enabled Historic England to confirm that it was Brown who designed the park at Hornby Castle on behalf of Robert D'Arcy, fourth Earl of Holdernesse, *c.*1765-1778, is published in *Yorkshire Capabilities* amidst the wealth of archive research compiled by Karen Lynch.[xxii] Chris Broughton's bird's-eye view (Figure 9) records the mansion as Brown would have seen it and the lakes under restoration above and below his rustic bridge cascade, and also unveils the other two lakes still overwhelmed by foliage. Compared with Neale's imagery of Harewood and Wentworth Castle, in which the trees are represented as a generic sylvan mass, it is clear that Broughton's overview articulates the modern appreciation of the rich variety of individual tree types. Like his Georgian predecessors, Broughton indulges in artistic licence and, most obligingly, reconstructs the derelict Bowling Green House and swivels it through ninety degrees so that the viewer can enjoy the entrance façade. His reconstruction is complemented by Catherine Aldred's companion drawing (Figure 10), which delineates the romantic overgrowth of park and ruin.

Through the country house portrait, the Georgian artist operated as a public relations consultant whose brief was to promote the landowner's social status and fashionable modernity. Within this genre, Turner's virtuoso invocation of oaken symbolism provided an additional *frisson* for patron and audience alike. Within this context, the artists illustrating *Yorkshire Capabilities* can be seen promoting the regenerative aims of heritage culture, recording the achievements of restoration and engaging with historical agendas that formerly were resolutely invisible.

Figure 9. Chris Broughton, *Brown at Hornby Castle,* **drawing for** *Yorkshire Capabilities: New Arcadian Journal 75/76,* **2016 (© the artist and the New Arcadian Press)**

Figure 10. Catherine Aldred, *Bowling Green House, Hornby Castle*, drawing for *Yorkshire Capabilities: New Arcadian Journal 75/76*, 2016 (© the artist and the New Arcadian Press)

[i] For the full version of Karen Lynch's research, see her 'Capability Brown in Yorkshire', in *Yorkshire Capabilities: New Arcadian Journal 75/76* (2016), pp. 37-107 (Temple Newsam, pp. 66-69); for the abridged version, see Karen Lynch, *Noble Prospects: Capability Brown and the Yorkshire Landscape* (Harrogate: Harrogate Borough Council and the Yorkshire Gardens Trust, 2016).

[ii] See John Phibbs, 'What went Wrong for Brown and what went Right', in *Yorkshire Capabilities: NAJ 75/76* (2016), pp. 24-35. See also, John Phibbs, 'A List of landscapes that have been attributed to Lancelot 'Capability' Brown', *Garden History*, vol. 41, no. 2 (2013), p. 274 (pp. 244-277) and vol. 42, no. 2 (2014), p. 286 (pp. 281-286).

[iii] Brown's first independent commissions were at Croome, Worcestershire, Petworth, Sussex, and Wotton, Buckinghamshire. See Richard Wheeler, 'Gardening and the Grenvilles: The Brownian Context at Wotton', in *The Grenville Landscape of Wotton House: New Arcadian Journal 65/66* (2009), pp. 39-49. Wotton is a triumph of Brown's water engineering (1750-1759), and this edition includes chapters by John Phibbs, Steffie Shields, Sarah Couch, Michael Symes, Michael Bevington, Michael Cousins, Kate Feluś and Patrick Eyres.

[iv] It is now well established that the first Earl fully understood the role of art in promoting the status and taste of an aristocratic dynasty, and that he applied this knowledge to the architecture and landscape of his Yorkshire estate between purchase in 1708 and his death in 1739. In so doing he was among the pioneers of the fashion for serpentine waterways during the 1730s. For Georgian Wentworth Castle, see

Patrick Eyres, Michael Charlesworth, Jan Woudstra, Chris Margrave, Jane Furse and Wendy Frith in *The Georgian Landscape of Wentworth Castle: New Arcadian Journal 63/64* (2nd edn., 2008); Charlesworth, Eyres and Furse in Patrick Eyres (ed.), *Wentworth Castle and Georgian Political Gardening: Jacobites, Tories and dissident Whigs* (Stainborough: Wentworth Castle Heritage Trust, 2012); Charlesworth, Eyres and Furse in Patrick Eyres and James Lomax (eds.), *Diplomats, Goldsmiths and Baroque Court Culture: Lord Raby in Berlin, The Hague and Wentworth Castle* (Stainborough: Wentworth Castle Heritage Trust, 2014); Patrick Eyres and Jane Furse, *Wentworth Castle Gardens: Guidebook* (Stainborough: Wentworth Castle Heritage Trust, 2014).

[v] For the second Earl's improvements, see Jane Furse in 'The Gothick and Picturesque Landscape of William Wentworth', in *The Georgian Landscape of Wentworth Castle: NAJ 63/64*, pp. 115-143. Note that the 1st edn., *NAJ 57/58* (2005), pp. 101-137, pre-dates the archive revelation about the Serpentine. Most of the Georgian landscape features survive, see Eyres and Furse, *Wentworth Castle Gardens*, pp. 13-22.

[vi] For discussion of Wentworth Castle's unlikely attribution to Brown, see Patrick Eyres, 'The Patriotism and Politics of Lancelot Brown's Capabilities', *Yorkshire Capabilities: NAJ 75/76*, pp. 142-153 (pp. 139-189).

[vii] For a detailed discussion, see Patrick Eyres, 'Commercial Profit and Cultural Display in the Eighteenth-Century Landscape Gardens at Wentworth Woodhouse and Harewood', in Michel Conan (ed.), *Bourgeois and Aristocratic Cultural Encounters in Garden Art, 1550-1850* (Washington DC: Dumbarton Oaks, 2002), pp. 189-219.

[viii] For Harewood, see Lynch (at n. 1), 'Capability Brown in Yorkshire', pp. 74-79.

[ix] See David Hill, *Turner in Yorkshire* (York: York City Art Gallery, 1980), *Turner in the North* (New Haven and London: Yale University Press, 1996), *Harewood Masterpieces: English Watercolours and Drawings* (Harewood: Harewood House Trust, 1995), and *Turner and Leeds: Image of Industry* (Huddersfield: Northern Arts Publications, 2008).

[x] For a broader discussion of this symbolism, see Patrick Eyres, 'Fleets, Forests and Follies: Supremacy of the Seas and of the Eye', *Hearts of Oak: New Arcadian Journal 35/36* (1993), pp. 8-23.

[xi] Dorothy Stroud, *Capability Brown* (London: Faber & Faber, 1975), p. 185.

[xii] See Eyres (at n. 6), 'The Patriotism and Politics', pp. 154-168.

[xiii] Madge Dresser and Andrew Hann (eds.), *Slavery and the British Country House* (Swindon: English Heritage, 2013), p. xiii.

[xiv] See Patrick Eyres, 'British Warfare and The Blackamoor: A Patriotic Celebration of Victory and Trade', *The Blackamoor & The Georgian Garden: New Arcadian Journal 69/70* (2011), pp. 25-95.

[xv] Dresser and Hann (at n. 13), *Slavery and the British Country House*, p. xiii.

[xvi] Simon Smith, *Slavery, Family, and Gentry Capitalism in the British Atlantic: The World of the Lascelles, 1648-1834* (Cambridge: Cambridge University Press, 2006).

[xvii] See also, David Lascelles, eighth Earl of Harewood, *Harewood: The Guidebook* (Harewood: Harewood House Trust, 2012), pp. 10-11.

[xviii] Wentworth Castle is an example and the connection with the Atlantic slave trade is explained in the guidebook; see Eyres and Furse (at n. 4), *Wentworth Castle Gardens*, p. 15. It is also detailed in Eyres (at n. 14), 'British Warfare and The Blackamoor', pp. 63-71.

[xix] For *Legacies of British Slave-ownership*, see <www.ucl.ac.uk/lbs/project>.

[xx] For Aske, see Lynch (at n. 1), 'Capability Brown in Yorkshire', pp. 72-76.

[xxi] See Michael Charlesworth, 'The Voyage of the Cannon Hall, 1755-1756', in *The Blackamoor and The Georgian Garden, NAJ 69/70* (2011), pp. 97-111.

[xxii] For Hornby, see Lynch (at n. 1), 'Capability Brown in Yorkshire', pp. 58-64.

Is ecology a barrier to the conservation of Brown's lakes?

Janet Fuller
University of Bath

Abstract

Capability Brown's lakes are an integral part of his design for English Landscape Parks, yet their conservation does not receive as much management attention as the other structural elements of these pastoral landscapes. One reason for this is the perceived misalignment between the ecological perspectives and the historical design aesthetic of these so-called "mirror" lakes. This has led to ecological and heritage conservationists often having conflicting priorities, adding cost and complexity to the challenge of managing these freshwater, artificial lakes.

This chapter explores the topic by considering the four most common misconceptions that have led to ecological issues being seen as a barrier to lake conservation. The discussion then turns to the practical issues of lake management by providing a framework for prioritising actions that takes into account both heritage and ecological considerations. Croome Park is included as a case study that provides examples of how this has been done.

The conclusions are that while ecological issues are often seen as a barrier to the historically-accurate conservation of Brown's lakes, the twin goals of ecological biodiversity and heritage conservation need not be mutually exclusive. The goal of improving water quality, so fundamental to maintaining ornamental lakes, should provide a commonality of purpose to unite ecologists and heritage conservationists. To work together, ecologists need to recognise ornamental lakes as an important part of wetland habitats, whilst heritage conservationists need to accept some degree of compromise in non-critical parts of a lake to allow a more natural appearance.

It should be noted that the term 'conservation' is used by both ecologists and historians. Here the words ''ecological conservation' and 'heritage conservation' are used where necessary to differentiate the two types of conservation. The term 'ecological value' is used to mean the ability (either existing or future) of a site to support habitats and species that are considered to be worthy of conserving, judged using criteria similar to those used for the Sites of Special Scientific Interest ("SSSI") designation. While the chapter is focussed on Brownian lakes, its conclusions apply to all historical, ornamental lakes. Most of the lakes in lowland England and in English Landscape Parks are shallow, nutrient-rich freshwater lakes and it is these characteristics that make the process of change, and therefore management, more complex.[1]

The Historical Perspective of Brown's Lakes in English Landscape Parks

Capability Brown is estimated to have created about 150 lakes.[2] Blenheim in Oxfordshire is often quoted as the finest of these water bodies. Some of his other commissions included Croome Park; Petworth; Sherborne Castle; Bowood; and Burton Constable. Capability's most recent biographer, Jane Brown, said "Of his sculptural materials – earth, trees and water – Lancelot had the most fun with water."[3] Another garden historian believed that "Brown's lakes and his treatment of water are his supreme achievement."[4]

Brown designed his lakes to be tranquil bodies of water that reflect the mansion, the sky and the surroundings. They are often referred to as "mirror lakes". They are a focal point of views from the mansion and in set-piece views as part of the circular tour of the estate as a 1758 painting of Croome Court [Figure 1] illustrates.

Figure 1. Croome Court, 1758 (Downloaded and reproduced from https://commons.wikimedia.org/wiki/File%3ARichard_Wilson_002.jpg [Accessed on 12/04/2016]).

The consensus view is that the banks of these lakes should be short grass, clear of any trees, shrubs and bankside vegetation. This is supported by eighteenth-century paintings as well as the criticism of Brown's minimalist approach that started at the end of the 1700s.[5] While this is true of the main views of the lake, some of Brown's lakes did have clumps of trees to make the lake appear to continue into the distance and to make separate lakes appear to be contiguous.

While a detailed consideration of eighteenth-century lake construction methods is beyond the scope of this paper, it is worth noting that Brown created lakes by one of three methods: constructing drains to collect and funnel water from the catchment area into a lake (Croome Park and Prior Park are both examples); by damming a river (as at Audley End); or by joining and expanding existing fish ponds (as at Burton Constable).

Even in the eighteenth century, the lakes needed ongoing management. For example, at Sherborne, "Brown's sluices were opened every year in November to let the water out into the channel below so that the labourers could go into the lake with wheelbarrows and scrape up the accumulated silt."[6]

Water Quality

The over-riding ecological goal is biodiversity, and ecologists agree that the "single most important factor for wetland biodiversity"[7] is good water quality. Therefore an understanding of the key requirements for water quality is necessary before discussing the ecological priorities for managing Brown's lakes. Heritage conservationists also want good water quality as clear water is more aesthetically consistent with mirror lakes, and algal blooms can be toxic with a rather unpleasant smell.[8]

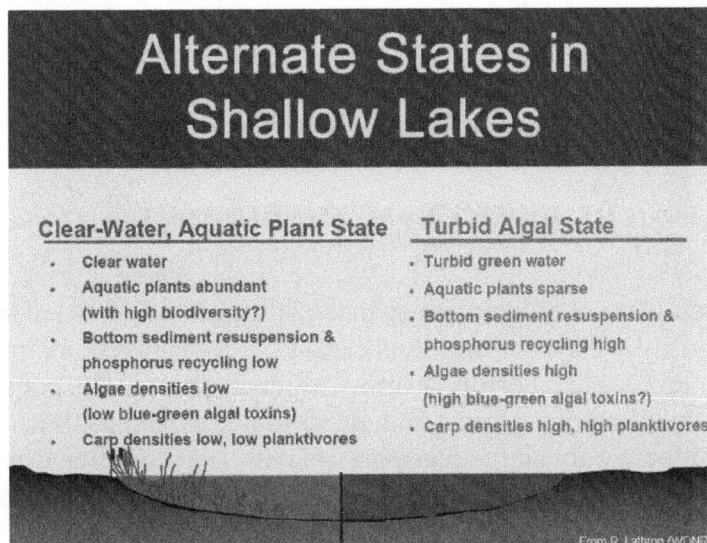

Alternate States in Shallow Lakes

Clear-Water, Aquatic Plant State	Turbid Algal State
• Clear water	• Turbid green water
• Aquatic plants abundant (with high biodiversity?)	• Aquatic plants sparse
• Bottom sediment resuspension & phosphorus recycling low	• Bottom sediment resuspension & phosphorus recycling high
• Algae densities low (low blue-green algal toxins)	• Algae densities high (high blue-green algal toxins?)
• Carp densities low, low planktivores	• Carp densities high, high planktivores

From R. Lathrop (WDNR)

Figure 2. Alternative Stable States in Shallow, Eutrophic lakes
(Reproduced from Osmon, 2008, Wisconsin Association of Lakes, p. 1.)

Clear water requires a nutrient loading that is balanced with the lake's biomass, an abundance of macrophytes, and low algae densities [Figure 2]. Macrophytes are aquatic plants visible to the naked eye and are a good indicator of water quality directly affecting the diversity of other species.[9] The opposite, turbid state is characterised by abundant phytoplankton and algal bloom. Phytoplankton are microscopic aquatic organisms that include algae and provide food for a wide range of aquatic animals. The shift from clear water to turbid occurs when there is an excess of phytoplankton.

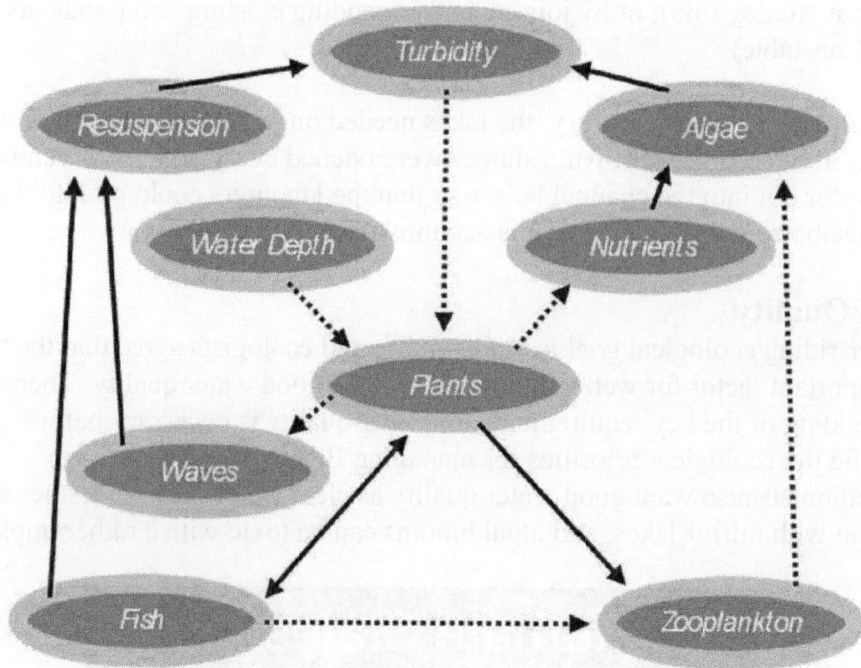

Figure 3 Shallow Lakes Management Model (Single-arrow solid lines = positive influence; Single-arrow dotted lines = negative influence; Double-arrow lines = either) Source: Modified from Scheffer et al. 1993

Figure 3. Example of a downward spiral into the Turbid State
(Reproduced from Osmon, 2008, p. 3)

There are a complex set of interactions that can trigger a downward spiral into the turbid state [Figure 3]. The two most important factors in preventing turbid water are low nutrient levels and a healthy quantity of macrophytes. The nutrients of concern are nitrogen and phosphorus in their various compounds. It is a useful simplification to focus only on the phosphorus levels as these often drive the growth in algal blooms because the phosphorus levels are too high for the amount of nitrogen. In addition, phosphorus levels entering the lake may be easier to reduce because the major sources are sewage treatment and intensive agriculture. In contrast, an increasing source of nitrogen entering lakes is from the atmosphere [Figure 4].

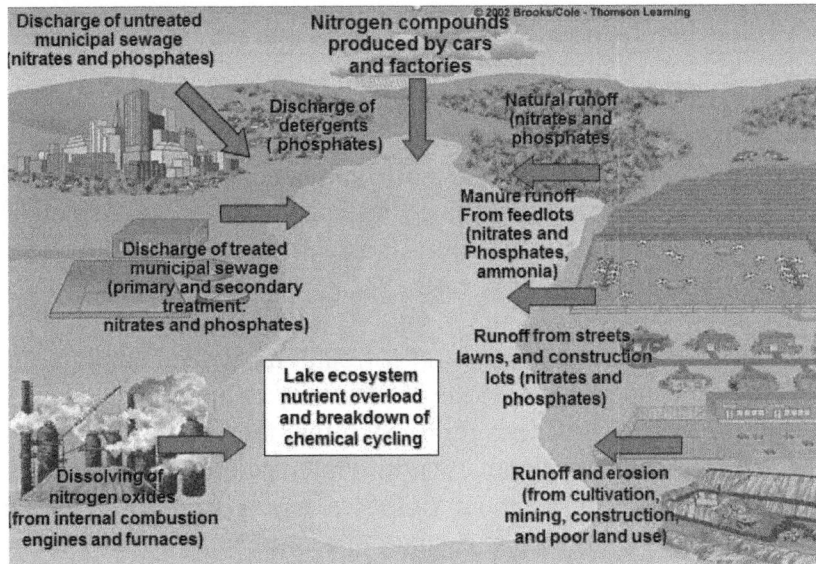

Figure 4. External Sources of Nutrient Enrichment to Lakes (Reproduced from http://www.slidefinder.net from home.dimedu.edu.cn [Accessed on 19th April 2016])

The Ecological Perspectives of the Value of Ornamental Lakes

The ongoing management of Brown's lakes has been hampered by a lack of understanding of what is required to maintain them; concerns about the cost and complexity of the task and the apparent incompatibility between heritage and ecological priorities. This latter point results in ecology being an unintended barrier to an historical lake's conservation. These misconceptions about current ecological priorities can be summarised into four categories.

1. Species versus Habitat Diversity

When it began, nature conservation was concerned primarily with species diversity. This is reflected in some of the current legislative requirements that had their origins in the 1980s and 1990s, such as the Wildlife and Countryside Act 1981 and the European Conservation (Habitats and Species) Regulations 2010. These regulations protect individual species such as great crested newts and bats.

There has been an increasing recognition over the last twenty-five years that species protection on its own is not sufficient, and more attention needs to be paid to habitats. The Lawton review, 'Making space for nature' published in 2010, recommended that England's ecological network needs to be *"more, bigger, better and joined"*[10] to stop the decline in biodiversity. Recent studies have stressed the need for an integrated approach to the management of the environment, and recognised that in England where space is limited, sites should have multiple purposes where possible.[11] The diversity of habitats within a connected network has been shown to be particularly important for wetlands.[12]

2. Lakes should be natural

One of the key criteria for judging the ecological value of a site is 'naturalness'[13]. This has led to ornamental lakes being largely overlooked by ecologists until recently. Naturalness should apply both to the appearance of a habitat as well as the ecological processes underlying it. It is a difficult concept in England, as all parts of the landscape have been affected by man. It has been noted that "Britain is largely a cultural landscape, and that human actions have had a pervasive influence on almost all of our ecosystems, habitats and species."[14]

It has been argued that there need be no correlation between naturalness and diversity.[15] The growing evidence of the biodiversity of man-made lakes, supports this view, with the recent guidelines for SSSI noting that many "old man-made lakes . . . have developed considerable wildlife interest, and ... have become important habitats in parts of the country otherwise poorly endowed with natural fresh water of a comparable type."[16] A study that compared the conservation value of shallow lakes in the Norfolk and Suffolk Broads[17] to ornamental lakes (primarily of the eighteenth and nineteenth centuries), concluded that "ornamental lakes are worthy of much greater attention from [nature] conservation organizations."[18]

A contributing factor for the lack of attention is the commonly-held view that once properly established, natural processes should be sufficient for lakes to need little ongoing management. For example, one well-respected book about historic landscape conservation suggests that turbid water is often a temporary state that will resolve itself as nature provides the "right balance of plants and animal life ... [to] absorb the algae."[19] As noted above, this is not necessarily correct and ongoing management of ornamental lakes is needed.

3. Reversion to the natural state

The other part of naturalness is the degree to which ecological processes are allowed to occur. In the past, it was felt that the act of restoring the open-water aspect of a lake negated its ecological value, and that an ornamental lake should be allowed to naturally infill, and be part of the successional process to become in time wet grasslands and then wet woodland.[20] The extreme version of this concept is re-wilding,[21] and it has tended to polarise views, widening the gap between ecologists and heritage conservationists.

It is now accepted that the ideal environment for biodiversity is to have a range of habitats at different successional states to maximise the variety of habitats available. In many situations, the role of the nature conservationist is to maintain a particular stage or series of stages of succession.[22] This integrated approach to habitat management should encompass the entirety of the freshwater, wetland complex including the floodplain, water bodies and flowing water".[23] Moreover, the linkages of the wetland "should be allowed to flow more naturally wherever possible".[24] For example, a lake that is allowed to flood in winter and have a reduced water level in summer is more likely to have a richer biodiversity than a lake for which the water level is kept relatively constant.

Another aspect of allowing processes to be natural is the difficult issue of management of aquatic vegetation in Brown's mirror lakes. The importance of having an abundant community of macrophytes for healthy water has been discussed. This is not necessarily compatible with maintaining a reflective surface of water. An ecologist at the National Trust said that mirror lakes are "a denial of natural processes, and even of nature itself, and that they were created before, and have no sustainable place in our age of ecological enlightenment."[25] The apparent conclusion is that it is not possible to maintain clear water in today's environment due to the high nutrient levels in the water, and it is not possible to reduce these sufficiently to allow only submerged vegetation. Given the importance of improving water quality generally, the heritage value of these lakes and their ecological value, this paper suggests that a thorough examination of what is achievable should be undertaken. As will be described, Croome Park has achieved a great deal in terms of nutrient reduction and clear water.

4. Dredging
Ecological concerns about dredging have been both principle-based, linked to the desire to have lakes naturally infill as part of the succession process and the belief that dredging should be avoided "as it can make water quality problems worse".[26] This is because dredging is a substantial disturbance of the sediment, resulting in a resuspension of phosphorus in the water column, a loss of aquatic plants and a potential loss of other wildlife. Yet when a lake is silted up, there is little choice but to dredge to restore the lake.

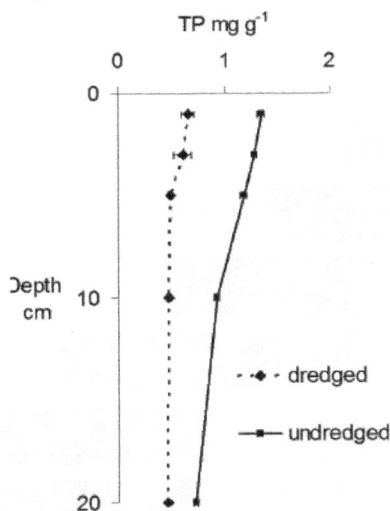

Figure 5. Total Phosphorus (TP) Concentration of the Barton Broad Sediment before and after dredging. (Used with permission from Kelly, 2008, p. 8.)

Dredging remains a subject for debate, although there is a converging view amongst ecologists that it is effective at improving the ecological health of a lake over the medium to long term when faced with a badly-silted lake with a history of heavy phosphorus loading.[27] For example, evidence from the Norfolk Broads shows that while dredging may make water quality worse in the first few months after it is completed, the longer term improvement in water quality justifies the effort. In particular, it reduced the significant amount of phosphorus that was being released into the water from the sediment [Figure 5].

Dredging can improve water quality but should be considered only after sources of silt and external nutrients have been reduced so that the need for large-scale dredging in the future is substantially reduced or eliminated. In addition, a thorough impact analysis should be done that considers all the issues connected with dredging including impact on wildlife, possible archaeological evidence in the sediments, method of dredging, spoil disposal and of course, cost.

Framework for Managing Brownian Lakes

This chapter suggests a framework to assist in decisions as to which management actions to take to restore historic lakes in poor health [Figure 6]. The focus of this framework is to establish sources of nutrient entering the lake and to reduce their inflows as much as possible to improve the water quality. The first step is to agree a lake management plan. This should describe the current status of the lake and the target situation, including specific targets for nutrient levels [Figure 7] and quantity of submerged plants, as well as providing a list of possible actions to be considered. Developing such a plan is recommended as it provides a clear direction and framework for management decisions, as well as providing the ability to measure progress.

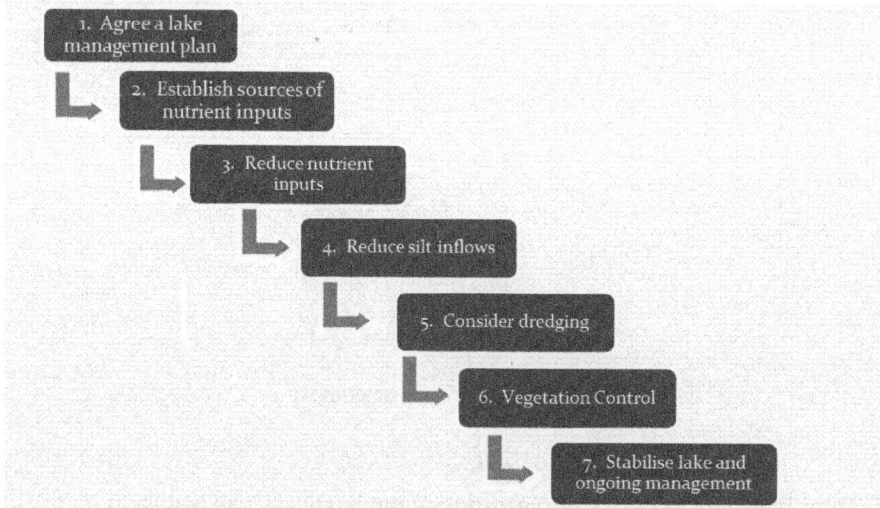

1. Agree a lake management plan
2. Establish sources of nutrient inputs
3. Reduce nutrient inputs
4. Reduce silt inflows
5. Consider dredging
6. Vegetation Control
7. Stabilise lake and ongoing management

Figure 6. Framework for Management Action to Restore a Brownian Lake

Nutrient	Recommended levels
Nitrogen	Mean annual levels no more than 1 milligram per litre.
Phosphorus	Annual mean total no more than .05 milligrams per litre
Oxygen	More than 5 milligrams per litre

Figure 7: Improving 2015 Recommended Nutrient Levels in Lakes and Ponds (Produced by author from consolidating information provided by Brunner, Hallas and Hector, 2015, p. 44 and Kelly, 2015, p. 5.)

The next step is to identify the source of the nutrients entering the lake, and where possible, the amount. Actions should then be taken to reduce these external nutrients entering the system. For example, where sewage is a source of nutrients, it is worthwhile working with water companies to encourage improvements in the sewage treatment of water entering the catchment area. Some sites have achieved a significant reduction in the phosphorus loading by this step alone, such as Loe Pool in Cornwall.[28]

Nutrients in a lake are affected also by various local factors. Common carp (*Cyprinus carpio*) can disturb the sediment that releases phosphorus back into the water. Large carp in particular "have been described as the fish equivalent of bulldozers"[29] because they do so much damage by uprooting aquatic plants and disturbing sediment. In very shallow lakes, wind can disturb the sediment. Excessive wildfowl can increase the nutrient loading from their excrement. Decaying vegetation also releases phosphorus back into the water.

Management of silt is important, both to reduce nutrient loading and to reduce the sediment building up in the lake. The extent of silting has become much more severe due to modern farming practices. Also, there is evidence that this problem is increasing as the soil becomes saturated with phosphorus and "much more is running off as soluble phosphorus than previously."[30] It is important therefore to work in partnership with farms in the catchment area to persuade them to change their farming practices.[31] Changes such as ploughing across slopes rather than down them; applying fertilizer in damp rather than wet weather and ploughing it in immediately; and re-instating field ponds and vegetation at the edge of fields all help.[32,33]

Another step to reduce silt is to provide buffer zones of wetland vegetation and install silt traps. Wetlands reduce the risk of flooding and drought by storing water, filter nutrients and silt, and provide a habitat for wildlife.[34] This is illustrated in the Croome Park case study which follows. Then dredging should be considered if the phosphorus levels remain above the target levels, or if the depth of the lake needs to be restored.

Vegetation control is a major problem for most man-made lakes as has been noted. Given the important role played by a buffer zone of vegetation around a lake, there is a conflict between this and the historical aesthetics of having clean-cut edges. It can be mitigated to some extent by leaving vegetation around portions of the lake which are not part of the key historic views and by maintaining other areas of wetlands. The Brownian technique of disguising the ends of his lakes also provides an opportunity for bankside vegetation.

Case Study: Croome Park

The case study of Croome Park provides an opportunity to describe the restoration work done on Brown's lakes in 2002 and 2003 and more importantly to judge its success today. Simon Barker, the Wildlife and Countryside Adviser for the west of the Midlands region, National Trust, will be presenting a separate study that describes the restoration work on the remainder of the landscape.

Croome was created for George William, 6th Earl of Coventry (1722–1809) by Capability Brown. It was Brown's first major commission in 1751 and he continued to work on it for the rest of his life Brown developed the artificial lake and river by draining the boggy ground as there was no natural river nearby.[35] The lake is approximately 1.8 hectares and the 1.7 km-long artificial river runs from the lake around the house and ends at a weir.[36] Katherine Alker, the Garden and Park Manager at Croome, describes the lake and river as a "big bath with a plug at the end".[37] This is an apt description as the lake collects the water from the catchment area, aided by the drainage system, and it snakes along the river to the carriage splash, small pond and weir. Figure 8 shows the park in 1796 soon after Brown's death.

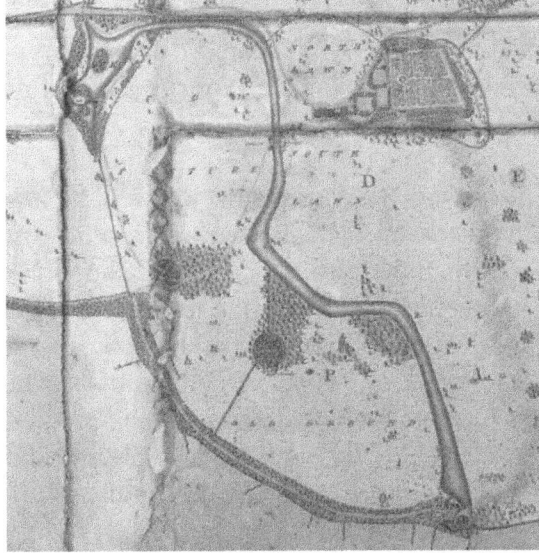

Figure 8: Detail of Snape's 1796 Map of Croome Park. (Reproduced with permission of the National Trust)

When the National Trust acquired Croome Park in 1996, the entire landscape was in very poor condition. There was a clear direction given for the restoration project that nothing less than a return to what had made Croome great in the eighteenth century would suffice.[38] This plan included the lake and river, using the 1758 image as one of the key views to recreate. Despite some ecological misgivings[39], three wetlands were created in 2002 and 2003 - Lickmoor, Snape and Menagerie [Figure 9]. These were developed to compensate for the dredging of the lake and river, which had become regionally-important reedbeds. The wetlands also filter out silt and nutrients from the agricultural land and pollutants from the nearby M5 motorway, and thereby improve the quality of the water flowing through to the lake and river.[40]

The original objectives of the project have been largely met.[41] Two of the three wetlands established quickly; Menagerie was slower possibly because it was too small an area.[42] A thorough nature conservation survey done in 2007 provided good evidence for the successful operation of these wetlands and the range of species supported.[43]

Another key role of the wetlands was to reduce the amount of silt and nutrients entering the lake and river. This has been partially successful. At Lickmoor, for example, there was a central pool designed to act as a silt trap to be dredged every five to ten years. The silt was removed in 2012, almost exactly ten years after establishment, and it was a much easier task than dredging the main lake.[44] Lickmoor is a large, shallow area (*circa* two hectares) and is good at nutrient capture. However, there is still more silt (and therefore presumably nutrients) entering the lake and river than hoped because there are two fields remaining within the parkland that are still intensely cultivated.[45] The rest of the parkland has now been returned to permanent pasture which is more consistent with the eighteenth-century estate's appearance, and has the additional benefit of reducing silt and nutrients entering the lake and river.

The importance of having a variety of connected wetland habitats in reasonably close proximity to each other; and allowing the water to flow more naturally was not explicitly recognised when the wetlands were created; nonetheless, the wetlands in Croome Park have achieved this. In addition to the lake, river and wetlands, there are ten ponds, which are lightly managed to provide a range of different habitats. For example, Pond 5 is regarded as "an important freshwater refuge on the estate – it is spring-fed, has some running water species, and has cool, deep shaded water not present in the other ponds."[46] The wetlands also provide the opportunity to allow the water to flow more naturally. The stream in the Menagerie wetland has been changed from a straight drain to a meandering water course.[47] The water is allowed to flood the land at Lickmoor, reinstating what is thought to be a natural wet woodland. This benefits the artificial lake and river by filtering the water of nutrients and silt, while contributing to biodiversity. It is felt that the water quality of the lake and river has improved, although it is only possible to assess water quality by visual inspection as there is no testing done of actual nutrient content. [48] There remains a small problem with blanket weed for about twenty days per year,[49] and barley straw is used to counteract it.

One of the biggest remaining issues is reed growth, particularly in the river. The stretch of the river from the lake to the Chinese Bridge has been dredged twice since the creation of the wetlands – once in 2008 and again in 2013.[50] This section has steep banks, has high visitor numbers and has no cattle grazing to assist in keeping the reeds under control [Figure 10]. In the lake, the reeds are dug out manually and are less of an issue.

The other major issue is the weir. It is deteriorating, and as a result of these concerns, the water level is being kept about 0.3m lower than it should be.[51] The reduced water level increases the problems of blanket weed and emergent vegetation. As the Reservoirs Act 1975 (modified by the Flood and Water Management Act 2010) applies to the lake and river, repairs will need to be done in accordance with its provisions increasing the cost and complexity of the work. In summary, it is encouraging that the creation of the wetlands has been largely successful at meeting the dual objectives of reducing the silt and nutrients entering the lake and re-establishing the reedbeds and their associated wildlife. They also have contributed to a large, connected and diverse area of wetland that does not detract in any way from the designed landscape. Despite positive results, issues remain and demonstrate the need for ongoing management of the ornamental lake and river.

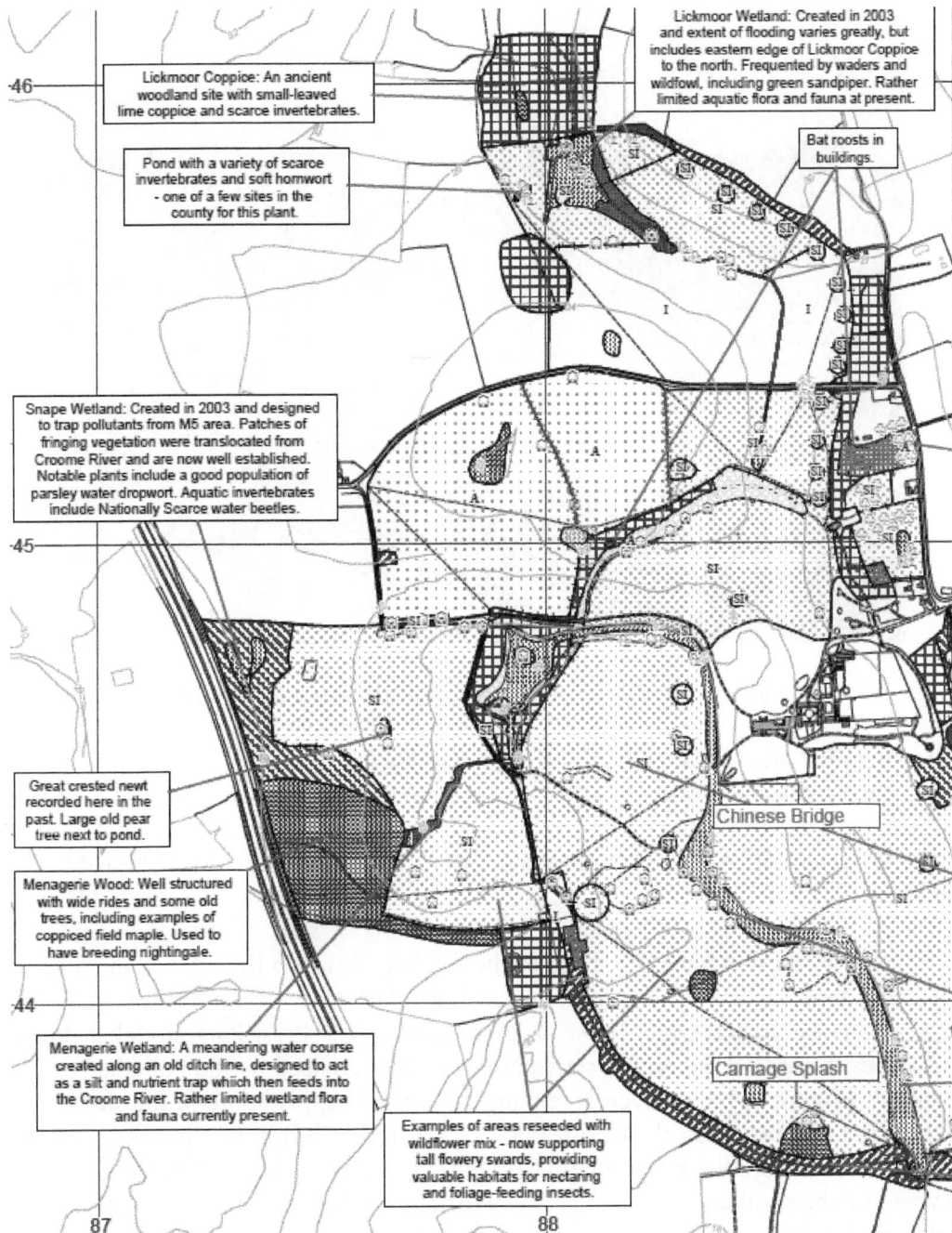

Figure 9: Map of Croome Park showing Location of Wetlands (Used with permission by the National Trust from Foster, Barker and Barker, 2009, p. 3. Note two additional labels have been added).

Figure 10. River between Chinese Bridge and Lake, July 2015

Site-specific Considerations with the Framework

The suggested framework is useful to set out the steps to be considered but there is "no single prescriptive approach" [52] Each site should have a management plan that takes into account its special significance, its circumstances and the achievable actions.

Not every site will have the space or the funds to develop linked wetland areas as has been done at Croome. For example, at Prior Park above Bath, it is not possible to re-introduce natural water flows, as there is no space. Prior Park stretches down the valley towards Bath, with a series of three lakes crossed by the Palladian Bridge[53] [Figure 11]. However, it remains possible to apply some of the steps. As part of the restoration work at Prior Park, an artificial silt trap was placed at the end of the drains before the water enters the Upper Lake [Figure 12]. It is cleared twice a year and the spoil kept on site. This is a different solution to Croome Park – a brick-built culvert rather than a natural wetland – but it is works well in this situation given the site constraints of a valley.

Figure 11. View of Palladian Bridge and Lakes, Prior Park (This photo of Prior Park Landscape Gardens (NT) is courtesy of TripAdvisor. Reproduced from www.tripadvisor.co.uk/LocationPhotoDirectLink-g186370-d213444-i174322107-Prior_Park_Landscape_Gardens_NT-Bath_Somerset_England.html#174322107 [Accessed on 21 April 2016])

There are many situations where there are conflicting priorities – one such example is managing fish populations. Bottom-feeding fish, particularly common carp, should be removed from ornamental lakes to improve the water quality. Unfortunately, they are also beloved of many angling clubs who may provide a source of needed revenue for historic parks.

Figure 12. Silt Trap at Prior Park, July 2015.

There are other issues that need to be considered as part of the complete management plan. For example, Canada geese (*Branta Canadensis*) do a lot of damage and their numbers need to be kept in check. Other invasive species include the signal crayfish (*Pacifastacus leniusculus*) that burrow into the banks of earth dams, potentially destabilising them. To date, it has proved impossible to control their spread. Australian swamp stonecrop (*Crassula helmsii*) is just one example of a number of alien, invasive aquatic plants for which there are no effective controls. Finally, mention needs to be made about legislation. Historic lakes are impacted by legislation that protects heritage assets, the natural environment, water, waste and health and safety. The legislation is often very specific and fragmented and fails to properly reflect the integrated needs of habitats. For example, the Reservoirs Act 1975 and the subsequent amending legislation in 2010 add significant responsibility and cost to maintaining dams and their associated infrastructure (such as weirs, overflow channels and valves). Dams also are barriers between habitats, inhibiting the natural flow of water through the landscape.

Conclusions

The recognition by ecologists that biodiversity is enhanced by connected wetland habitats at different successional stages negates the apparent ecological barriers to the restoration and ongoing management of historical ornamental lakes. Despite the fact such lakes are man-made features in highly-managed landscapes, they can be a valuable part of the wetland habitat.

Mirror lakes are an essential part of Brown's nationally-significant English Landscape Parks, and a thorough, integrated approach is needed to manage the complex interactions that affect the health of these lakes. The common objective for ecological and heritage conservation should be to maximise ecological potential within the constraints dictated by the historical appearance of the critical areas, with a more ecologically-friendly regime in the wider landscape. At a practical level, improving water quality is a shared objective of both ecologists and heritage conservationists and should provide a consensus for management actions.

End notes

[1] Moss, Madgwick and Phillips, 1996, p. 17.

[2] Brown, 2011, p. 131.

[3] Brown, 2011, p. 83.

[4] Thacker, 1994, p. 218.

[5] See for example Ross, 1987, p. 274.

[6] Waymark, 2001, p. 69.

[7] Webb, Drewitt and Measures, 2010, p. 9.

[8] Barrow, 2014. Certain types of blue-green algae (called cyanobacteria) can produce toxins that can kill pets and cause human illness.

[9] Sayer, 2015, pers. comms.

[10] Lawton *et al*, 2010, p. viii. Italics in original.

[11] Hearn and Thompson, 2012, p. 329.

[12] Countryside Survey, 2010, p. 53.

[13] Bainbridge *et al.*, 2013, p. 3.

[14] Bainbridge *et al.*, 2013, p. 24.

[15] Margules and Usher, 1981, p. 93.

[16] Joint Nature Conservation Committee, n.d., p. 2.

[17] It is interesting to note that the Norfolk and Suffolk Broads, while largely considered today to be natural, were created from flooded peat workings in the twelfth to fourteenth centuries.

[18] Sayer, Davidson and Kelly, 2008, p. 1051.

[19] Watkins and Wright, 2008, p. 192.

[20] Hearn, 2008a, p. 6.

[21] The re-introduction of the beaver is an example of re-wilding.

[22] Hodd, 2015, pers. comm.

[23] Webb, Drewitt and Measures, 2010, p. 52.

[24] National Trust, 2008a, p. 24.

[25] Oates, 2001, p. 133.

[26] Hearn, 2008a, p. 4.

[27] Sayer, 2015, pers. comm..

[28] National Trust, 2008a, p. 23. Loe Pool is Cornwall's largest natural lake.

[29] Moss, Madgwick and Phillips, 1996, p. 70.

[30] Moss, Madgwick and Phillips, 1996, p. 78.

[31] The Catchment Sensitive Farming Initiative, run by Natural England, is one such scheme. See https://www.gov.uk/guidance/catchment-sensitive-farming-reduce-agricultural-water-pollution.

[32] Moss, Madgwick and Phillips, 1996, p. 83.

[33] Hearn, Flanders and Phillips, 2002, p. 12.

[34] Hearn, 2008a, p. 2.

[35] Gordon noted that the artificial river was completed in 1748 probably by Sanderson Miller. However, Brown changed it to make it more naturalistic and curve around the house. See Gordon, 2000, p. 104.

[36] Foster, Barker and Barker, 2009, p. 24.

[37] Alker, 2015, pers. comm.

[38] Haycock, 2015, pers. comm.

[39] Hearn, Flanders and Phillips, 2002, p. 15.

[40] Oates, 2001, pp. 142 – 145.

[41] Barker, 2015, pers. comm.

[42] Haycock, 2015, pers. comm.

[43] Foster, Barker and Barker, 2009, p. 29.

[44] Alker, 2015, pers. comm.

[45] Barker, 2015, pers. comm.

[46] Foster, Barker and Barker, 2009, p. 33.

[47] Alker, 2015, pers. comm.

[48] Barker, 2015, pers. comm.

[49] Haycock, 2015, pers. comm.

[50] Alker, 2015, pers. comm.

[51] Alker, 2015, pers. comm.

[52] Moss, Madgwick and Phillips, 1996, p. 17.

[53] There are only two other such bridges in England – one at Stowe and one at Wilton, Wiltshire.

Bibliography

References

Anon. (2014a) *Guide to Understanding Freshwater Aquatic Plants*. Rhode Island Department of Environmental Management, Rhode Island, USA.

Anon. (2014b) Freshwater Ecology. *Inpractice*, Issue **84**, June 2014. Chartered Institute of Ecology and Environmental Management.

Bainbridge, I., Brown, A., Burnett, N., Corbett, P., Cork, C., Ferris, R., Howe, M., Maddock, A., Mountford, E., & Pritchard, S. (eds) (2013) *Guidelines for the Selection of Biological SSSIs.* Joint Nature Conservation Committee. Available at: www.jncc.defra.gov.uk/page-2303 [Accessed on 13 August 2015].

Barker, S. (2006) *The Croome Restoration and Wildlife*. National Trust. Unpublished report (personal communication, 29 May 2015).

Barker, S., n.d. *Croome Park: Wet Water Meadow & Woodland Management Scheme*. National Trust. [pdf] (Personal communication, 29 May 2015).

Bending, S. (1992) Re-reading the eighteenth-century landscape garden. *Huntingdon Library Quarterly*, **55** (3), 379-99.

Bettess, R., Fisher, K., Hardwick, M., Holmes, N., Mant, J., Sayers, P., Sear, D., & Thorne, C. (2011) *Key Recommendations for sediment management – A Synthesis of River Sediments and Habitats (Phase 2).* Bristol: Environment Agency.

Binnie, G., 1987. *Early Dam Builders in Britain*. Thomas Telford, London.

Boylan, J. (2001) *Advancements in Determining the Role of Barley Straw*. [pdf] Available at: http://extension.psu.edu/natural-resources/water/ponds/pond-management/aquatic-plants/barleystrawsynopsis.[Accessed on 19 July 2015].

Brown, J. (2011) *The Omnipotent Magician: Lancelot 'Capability' Brown 1716-1783.* Chatto and Windus, London.

Brunner, P., Hallas, A., & Hector, J. (2015) *Sediment Removal Feasibility Study: Bosherston Lakes, Stackpole Pembrokeshire, Wales*. Royal Haskoning DHV and National Trust unpublished report (personal communication, 20 July 2015).

Cathersides, A., Wells, D., & Parker, E. (2014a) *Landscape Advice Note: Canada Geese*. English Heritage, London.

Cathersides, A., Wells, D., & Parker, E. (2014b) *Landscape Advice Note: Conservation of Aquatic Habitats*. London: English Heritage

Cohen, M. (ed.) (2005) *Dredging: The Facts.* Available at: https://www.iadc-dredging.com/ul/cms/fck-uploaded/documents/PDF%20Publications/dredging-literature-dredging-the-facts.pdf [Accessed 31 March 2014]

Communities and Local Government (2012) *National Planning Policy Framework.* The Stationery Office, London.

Cooper, G., & Taylor, G. (1987) *English Water Gardens*. Weldenfeld and Nicholson, London.

Countryside Survey (2007) *England Results, 2007*. Available at: http://www.countrysidesurvey.org.uk/outputs/england-results-2007 [Accessed on 26 June 2015].

Countryside Survey (2010) *Ponds Report from 2007*. Available at: http://www.countrysidesurvey.org.uk/outputs/ponds-report-from-2007 [Accessed on 20 July 2015].

Currie, C. (1990) Fishponds as Garden Features, *c.* 1550 – 1750. *Garden History*, **18**, No. 1, pp. 22 – 46.

Daniels, S. (2000) *Humphrey Repton: Landscape Gardening and the Geography of Georgian England*. Yale University Press, New Haven and London.

Duker, L. & Palmer, M. (2009) Methods for assessing the conservation value of lakes. In: *Assessing the Conservation Value of Freshwaters*. Cambridge University Press, Cambridge, pp. 166 - 199.

Eburne, A. & Taylor, R. (2006) *How to Read an English Garden*. London: Ebury Press.

Environment Agency, 2010. *Creating a Better Place. The Owner's Guide to Reservoir Safety*. Bristol: Environment Agency.

Environment Agency, n.d. *A Better Place to Live. Working Together for the Safety of our Reservoirs*. Environment Agency, Bristol.

Felus, K. (2006) Boats and Boating in the Designed Landscape, 1720 – 1820. *Garden History*, **34**, No. 1, 22-46.

Fielden, K. (2010) *Bowood House and Gardens*. Heritage House Group, Norwich.

Fisher, R. (1993) Biological Aspects of the Conservation of Wetlands. In: *Conservation in Progress*. John Wiley and Sons Ltd, Chichester, pp. 97 - 113.

Foster, A., Barker, S. & Barker, G. (2009) *Nature Conservation Evaluation. Croome Park, Worcestershire. 2007 Survey*. National Trust unpublished document (personal communication, 13 July 2015).

Freshwater Habitats Trust (2013) *Report of the Workshop on the Protection and Management of Small Water Bodies. Brussels, 14 November, 2013*. Freshwater Habitats Trust, Oxford.

Fuller, J. (2014) *Case Study: Understanding the Water Features at Wrest Park and the Implications for their Conservation*. Unpublished MSc Coursework, University of Bath, Bath.

Garnett, O. (2008) *Croome Park*. National Trust, Swindon.

Gobster, P., Narsauer, J., Daniel, T. & Fry, G. (2007) The Shared Landscape: What does aesthetics have to do with ecology? *Landscape Ecology*, **22**, No. 7, 959 - 972.

Gordon, C. (2000) *The Coventrys of Croome*. Phillimore and Co. Ltd, Chichester.

Gregory, J., Spooner, S., & Williamson, T. (2013) *Lancelot 'Capability' Brown: A Research Impact Review Prepared for English Heritage by the Landscape Group, University of East Anglia.* English Heritage.

Hall, E. (1995) Mr. Brown's Directions': Capability Brown's Landscaping at Burton Constable (1767 – 82). *Garden History*, **23**, No. 2, pp. 145 - 174.

Hannan, H. (2014) A celebration of Capability Brown. In: *Landscape*, Autumn 2014. [Online]

Haycock, N., Evans, A. & White, J. (2013) *Landscape Advice Note: Historic parks and gardens and changes to reservoir safety legislation.* English Heritage, London.

Hazell, Z. & Robinson, D.E. (2001) *Moats, Ponds and Ornamental Lakes in the Historic Environment.* English Heritage, London.

Hearn, K. (2008a) *Conservation Directorate Guidance Note: Management of Lakes and Water Resources in Historic Parks. HP7 (2008).* Swindon: The National Trust.

Hearn, K. (2008b) *Vegetation Survey of Upper, Middle and Lower Lakes, Prior Park, Bath.* National Trust. [unpublished document] (Personal communication, 13 July 2015).

Hearn, K., Flanders, J., & Phillips T. (eds) (2002) *Sediment management and dredging in lakes. Report based on a workshop at Arlington Court, Devon, March 2002.* The National Trust, unpublished.

Hearn, K. & Thompson, T. (2012) *Delivering Ecosystem Services in National Trust Landscapes: Developing a Land Capability Process.* Soilscapes.

Herrington, S. (2010) The nature of Ian McHarg's Science. *Landscape Journal*, **29**, No.1, 1 - 10.

Hinde, T. (1986) *Capability Brown - The Story of a Master Gardener.* Hutchinson, London.

Hunt, J.D. (2000) *Greater Perfections: The Practice of Garden Theory.* Thames and Hudson, London.

Hunt, J.D. and Willis, P. (eds) (1988) *The Genius of the Place. The English Landscape 1620 – 1820.* MIT Press, London.

Hussey, C. (1967) *The Picturesque: studies in a point of view.* 3rd ed. Frank Cass and Company Ltd, London.

Hussey, C. (1946a) A Geordian Arcady: William Kent's Gardens at Rousham, Oxfordshire. *Country Life,* June 14, 1084 - 1087.

Hussey, C. (1946b) A Geordian Arcady: William Kent's Gardens at Rousham, Oxfordshire. *Country Life,* June 21, 1130 - 1133.

Jellicoe, G. & Jellicoe, S. (1971) *The Use of Water in Landscape Architecture.* London: Adam and Charles Black.

Joint Nature Conservation Committee, n.d. *Guidelines for the selection of biological SSSI's. Part 2: Detailed guidelines for habitats and species groups. Chapter 6 Freshwater Habitats.* JNCC, Peterborough.

Kay, S. (2012) *Croome Redefined. Conservation Management and Maintenance Plan.* National Trust.

Keddy, P.A. (2010) *Wetland Ecology.* Cambridge University Press, Cambridge.

Kelly, A. (2008) *Review of Sediment Removal. Appendix 3 Broads Lake Restoration Strategy.* Broads Authority, Norwich.

Kelly, A. (2015) *Summary Report: A review of lake restoration practices and their performance in the Broads National Park 1980 – 2013.* Broads Authority, Norwich.

Laird, M. (1999) *The Flowering of the Landscape Garden. English Pleasure Grounds 1720 – 1800.* University of Pennsylvania Press, Philadelphia.

Lawton, J., Brotherton, P., Brown, V., Elphick, C., Fitter, A., Forshaw, J., Haddow, R., Hiblorne, S., Leafe, R., Mace, G., Southgate, M., Sutherland, W., Tew, T., Varley, J., & Wynne, G. (2010) *Making Space for Nature: a review of England's wildlife sites and ecological network.* Report to Defra, Bristol.

Lewis, V., & Walsingham, M. (2006a) *The Management of Freshwater Fisheries.* National Trust, Swindon.

Lewis, V., & Walsingham, M. (2006b) *National Trust Fisheries Policy (Draft v4.0).* National Trust, Swindon.

Margules, C. & Usher, M.B. (1981) Criteria Used in Assessing Wildlife Conservation Potential: A Review. *Biological Conservation,* **21**, 79 - 109.

McHarg, I. (1971) *Design with Nature*. Doubleday and Company Inc, New York.

McParland, C. & Barrett, O. (2009) *Hydromorphological Literature Reviews for Lakes*. Environment Agency, Bristol.

Meir, J. (2002) Development of a natural style in designed landscapes between 1730 and 1760: the English Midlands and the work of Sanderson Miller and Lancelot Brown. *Garden History*, **30**, No. 1, 24 - 48.

Misiewicz, L. (2010) *Ecological Survey of Painshill Park*. Unpublished.

Monbiot, G. (2014) *Feral: Rewilding the Land, Sea and Human Life*. Penguin, London.

Moss, B., Madgwick, J. & Phillips, G. (1996) *A guide to the restoration of nutrient-enriched shallow lakes*. Environment Agency and Broads Authority, Norwich.

National Trust (2004) *Croome Park Monitoring 2004*. Unpublished.

National Trust (2007) *Views: Water*. Issue 44, September 2007.

National Trust (2008a) *From Source to Sea: working with water*. National Trust, Swindon.

National Trust (2008b) *Nature and the National Trust*. Swindon: National Trust.

Natural England (2011) *The Management of problems caused by Canada geese: a guide to best practice. Natural England Technical Information Note TIN009*. Natural England, Peterborough.

Natural England (2013) *The contribution of historic designed landscapes to ecosystem services*. Natural England, Peterborough.

Oates, M. (2001) Ecology and Nature Conservation in Gardens and Parks. In: *Rooted in History – Studies in Garden Conservation*. National Trust, London, pp. 125 - 145.

Osmon, D. (2008) An overview of shallow lakes ecology and management techniques. *The Lake Connection*, summer and fall editions, Wisconsin Association of Lakes.

Painshill Park Trust (2011) *Conservation Management Plan*. Painshill Park Trust, Cobham.

Painshill Park Trust (2010) *Painshill reborn: The Guide*, 2010. Painshill Park Trust, Cobham.

Palmer, M. (2008) *Plants of British standing waters: A conservation fact file*. Joint Nature Conservation Committee, Peterborough.

Peay, S. (2001) *Eradication of alien crayfish populations*. Environment Agency, Bristol.

Phibbs, J. (2003) The Englishness of Lancelot 'Capability' Brown. *Garden History*, **31**, Issue 2, 122 - 140.

Phibbs, J. (2010) The Structure of the Eighteenth-Century Garden. *Garden History*, **38**, No. 1, 20 - 34.

Plumptre, G. (2003) *The Water Garden*. London: Thames and Hudson.

Podolak, K., Kondolf, G. M., Mozingo, L. A., Bowhill, K., & Lovell, M. (2013) "Designing with Nature? The persistence of Capability Brown's 18th century water features." *Landscape Journal: design, planning and management of the land*, **32**, Number 1, 51-64.

Quest-Ritson, C. (2003) *The English Garden: A Social History*. David R. Godine, Boston.

Rackham, O. (2000) *The History of the Countryside*. (Re-print) Phoenix, London.

Randall, R., Drake, A., & Cenac II, W. (2011) Improvements for Dredging and Dredged Material Handling. *Proceedings, WEDA XXXI Technical Conference and TAMU 42 Dredging Seminar*.

Roberts, J. (2000) Stephen Switzer and water gardens. In: Ridgway, C., & Williams, R. (eds) (2000) *Sir John Vanbrugh and Landscape Architecture in Baroque England 1690 – 1730*. Sutton, Stroud.

Roberts, J. (2001) Well Temper'd Clay: Constructing Water Features in the Landscape Park. *Garden History*, **29**, No. 1, 12 – 28.

Ross, J. (1987) The Picturesque: an eighteenth-century debate. *Journal of Aesthetics and Art Criticism*, **46**, No. 2, 271 – 279.

Sayer, C. (2014) Conservation of aquatic landscapes: ponds, lakes, and rivers as integrated systems. *WIREs Water,* **1**, 573 - 585.

Sayer, C., Davidson, T. & Kelly, A. (2008) Ornamental Lakes – An overlooked Conservation Resource. *Aquatic Conservation Marine Freshwater Ecosystems*, **18**, Issue 6, 1046 - 1051.

Sayer, C., Burgess, A., Kari, K., Davidson, T., Peglar, S., Yang, H., & Rose, N. (2010) Long-term dynamic of submerged macrophytes and algae in a small and shallow, eutrophic lake: implications for the stability of macrophyte-dominance. *Freshwater Biology*, **55**, 565 – 583.

Sayer, C., Shilland, E., Greaves, H., Dawson, B., Patmore, I., Emson, D., Alderton, E., Robinson, P., Andrews, K., Axmacher, J., & Wiik, E. (2014) Managing Britain's ponds – conservation lessons from a Norfolk farm. *British Wildlife*, **26**, October, 21 - 28.

Shields, S. (2006) Mr Brown engineer': Lancelot Brown's early work at Grimsthorpe Castle and Stowe. *Garden History*, **34**, Issue 2, 174 - 191, plates I-XI.

Shields, S. (2011) *Conference Report: Historic Landscapes and the 2010 Flood and Water Management Act*.

Stebbing, P., Longshaw, M., Taylor, N., Norman, R., Lintott, R., Pearce, F., & Scott, A. (2012) *Review of methods for the control of invasive crayfish in Great Britain.* CEFAS Contract – Final Report C5471. CEFAS, Lowestoft.

Stroud, D. (1975) *Capability Brown*. Faber and Faber, London.

Symcs, M. (2000) *Mr. Hamilton's Elysium. The Gardens at Painshill.* Frances Lincoln Ltd, London.

Thacker, C. (1994) *The Genius of Gardening.* Weidenfeld and Nicolson, London.

Tree Associates (2012) *Case Study. Wotton House, Wotton Underwood, Aylesbury, Buckinghamshire.*

Turner, T. (2005) *Garden History. Philosophy and Design 2000 BC – 2000AD.* Taylor & Francis, London.

Ward, T. (2009) *Prior Park Landscape Garden*. National Trust, Swindon.

Warren, A. (1993) Naturalness: A Geomorphological Approach. In: *Conservation in Progress*. John Wiley and Sons Ltd, Chichester, pp. 15 - 24.

Watkins, J. & Wright, T. (eds) (2008) *The Management and Maintenance of Historical Parks, Gardens and Landscapes: the English Heritage Handbook*. Frances Lincoln, London.

Waymark, J. (2001) Sherborne Dorset. Lancelot Brown (1716 – 1783) and the Landscape Park. *Garden History*, **29**, Issue 1, 64 – 81.

Webb, J., Drewitt, A., & Measures, G. (2010) *Managing for species: Integrating the needs of England's priority species into habitat management. Part 1 Report*. Natural England Research Reports, Number 024, Peterborough.

Whately, T., 1777. *Observations on Modern Gardening*. 4th ed. T. Payne and Son, London.

Williamson, T. (1998) *Polite Landscapes: Gardens and Society in Eighteenth-Century England*. Sutton Publishing Limited, Stroud.

Wilson, M. (1984) *William Kent*. Routledge and Kegan Paul, London.

Wood, S. & Pratt, C. (2013) *Biological Control of Invasive Aquatic Plants. RINSE Best Practice Workshop, 17 October, 2013 Norwich*. CABE.

Zhang, S., Zhou, Q., Xu, D., Lin, J., Cheng, S., & Wu, Z. (2010) Effects of sediment dredging on water quality and zooplankton community structure in a shallow of eutrophic lake. *Journal of Environmental Science (China)*, **22**(2), 218 - 224.

Websites
Attar, R. & Mowl, T. (2010) The English Landscape Garden. *Historyextra*, [blog] 16 August 2010. Available at: http://www.historyextra.com/feature/english-landscape-garden [Accessed on 9 July 2015].
Barrow, T. (2014) *Toxic Algae Fact Sheet and Frequently Asked Questions*. University of Nebraska – Lincoln. [website] Available at: http://water.unl.edu/lakes/toxicalgae-faqs/ [Accessed on 30 August 2015].
Carpenter, S.R. and Cottingham, K.L. (1997) Resilience and Restoration of lakes. *Conservation Ecology* [online]. Available at: http://www.ecologyandsociety.org/vol1/iss1/art2/#PR [Accessed on 5th June 2015].
Environment Agency (2014) *Waste exemption: disposing of waste*. [website] Available at: https://www.gov.uk/waste-exemptions-disposing-of-waste [Accessed on 9 July 2015].
Ferguson, A. (2015) *RENEW Project*. [website] Available at: http://www.sheffield.ac.uk/cbe/research/renew [Accessed on 12 August 2015].

Forestry Commission England, 2015. *Heathland on the Forestry Commission Estate in England.* [website] Available at: http://www.forestry.gov.uk/england-heathland [Accessed on 30 August 2015].

Hobbs, R. & Norton, D. (1996) Towards a Conceptual Framework for Restoration Ecology. *Restoration Ecology*, **4**, No. 2, 93 – 110. [online] Available at: http://onlinelibrary.wiley.com/doi/10.1111/j.1526-100X.1996.tb00112.x/abstract [Accessed on 9 July 2015].

Moss, B. (2004) Ecological Engineering and the Restoration of Lakes. In: *Sherkin Comment*, Issue No. 37 [online] Available at: http://www.sherkinmarine.ie/SherkinComment37.pdf [Accessed on 23 June 2015].

Natural England (2015) *Catchment Sensitive Farming: reduce agricultural water pollution.* [website] Available at: https://www.gov.uk/guidance/catchment-sensitive-farming-reduce-agricultural-water-pollution [Accessed on 31 August 2015].

National Trust (2015) *What We Do.* [website] www.nationaltrust.org.uk/what-we-do [Accessed on 23 August 2015].

Podolak, K., n.d. *Capability Brown's Water Designs.* [blog]. Available at: https://capabilitybrown.wordpress.com/https://capabilitybrown.wordpress.com/ [Accessed on 23 June 2015].

Woods, M. (2010) *Pond Plants and Wildlife.* [Online] Available at: http://www.buildingconservation.com/articles/ponds/ponds.htm [Accessed on 5 June 2015].

Personal Communications

Alker, K. (2015) [Interview] (Personal communication, 31 July 2015).

Barker, S. (2015) [Email] (Personal communication, 26 July 2015).

Cathersides, A. (2015) [Email] (Personal communication, 22 June 2015)

Clarke, S. (2015) [Interview] (Personal communication, 20 July 2015)

Ebdon, M. (2015) [Interview] (Personal communication, 7 July 2015).

Exelby, E. (2015) [Email] (Personal communication, 4 August 2015).

Harney, M. (2015) [Email] (Personal communication, 23 March 2015)

Haycock, N. (2015) [Interview] (Personal communication, 31 July 2015).

Hodd, D. (2015) [Discussion] (Personal communication, 29 June 2015}

Leather, C. (2015) [Interview] (Personal communication, 7 August 2015).

Sayer, C. (2015) [Interview] (Personal communication, 5 August 2015).

Ward, M., Goulding, R., & Boden, T. (2015) [Interview] (Personal communication, 24 July 2015).

This work is based on the author's dissertation for her Master of Science in the Conservation of Historic Gardens and Cultural Landscapes at the University of Bath, September, 2015.

Blessed Brown and Biodiversity

Ted Green MBE
Founder President of the Ancient Tree Forum

The paintings in the caves at Altamera in northern Spain (Figure 1) accurately depict some of the large animals that roamed across Europe 14,000 years ago. Auroch, Elk, Bison, Exmoor Ponies, Reindeer and Red Deer. Today, it is widely recognised that these large grazing and browsing animals were not any part of the out-dated perception of a Europe covered with dark dense forest with little or no food for such animals. They were animals of an open expansive landscape of savanna parkland with herb-rich meadows, marsh, scrub, open grown trees of all ages and groves of varying size and age. So where best to see and experience today such a scene resembling 14,000 years ago other than our New Forest and in the historic landscape parks of Brown, Repton and other great landscapers? Their vision when planning these parks of leaving some ancient, veteran and over-mature trees along with some existing ancient meadows was to the ecologist of today one of the greatest contributions to environmental conservation known to Western man. Equal in importance to the national parks of the USA. By leaving these ancient trees and meadows and incorporating the already exsisting ancient deer parks, Brown and others created a landscape not only an analogue of the past but provided biological continuity for whole communities of species, these ancient individual organisms themselves are gene banks as yet untapped by scientists and are waiting the time for study for science does not stand still. In fact, these Brown landscapes and others could be termed Europe's rainforest and their fundamental importance outside the landscape world yet to be recognised.

Such landcapes are loved, admired, and studied by people throughout the world of tree people, historians, conservationists, environmentalists, ecologists, historic landscape architects. There is a distinct thread that brings people together are the trees of Brown and his colleagues.

In the designed landscape, trees with herb-rich meadows are essential and It could be argued that their conservation where possible with the original individual trees and the whole landscape is fundamental and of paramount importance by providing further biological continuity. Unfortunately over time, many of the original trees have been lost and sadly the use of large areas of land changed to other uses.

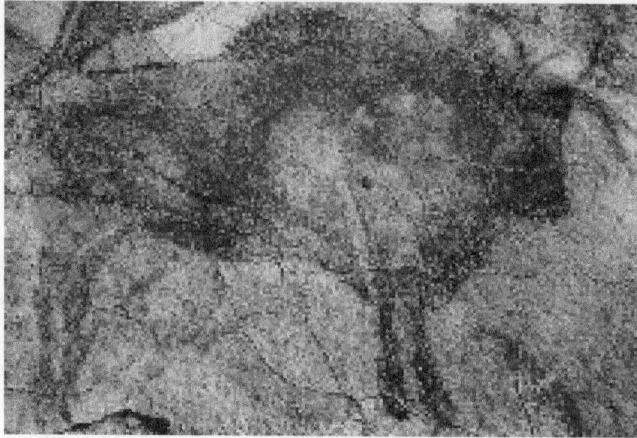

Figure 1. Cave painting of an Auroch at Altamera. One could say Frans Vera's landscapes of those large animals have been shown today to not only be able to maintain the landscape but create it in the process

Old, wide-spreading, open-grown trees, scrub and ancient pasture with an ancient breed of cow, a longhorn, could be said to be an analogue for the Auroch (Figure 2). The communities above and below ground present in these ancient wood pastures date back to the end of the Ice Age.

Figure 2. The picture describes the scene perhaps 14,000 years ago or today in some landscaped areas of the UK only 14 hours ago

Ancient Oak (Figure 3) is absolutely priceless for its gene banks that are concentrated in one individual tree never re-aggregated and lost elsewhere by natural selection through time. Its gene bank and the centuries-old biological continuity visible and invisible, above and below ground, make these ancient's importance fundamental. Without those landscapers, would this tree have remained?

Figure 3. An ancient Oak, well over 500 years old that remains in a landscaped park

Figure 4. A cartoon of an open-grown landscaped tree with some of its essential partners, the microorganisms, showing the relative volume and mass of the different components

A tree is a unique, dynamic, individual and mutualistic support system for fungi and other microorganisms. The cartoon representation of an open-grown tree (Figure 4) with some of its essential partners shows the sheer size and volume of the microorganisms that dwarf the tree's above-ground size and volume and are fundamental in maintaining the health of their soil. These reservoirs of gene banks and biodiversity are so important to conserve until science catches up. In most situations we have the great landscapers to thank for the conservation of these old trees in the landscape.

The Tamworth pigs are only rootling the ancient footpath which was never ploughed when the fields on either side were intensively farmed arable with fertiliser, pesticides and herbicides for many years (Figure 5). The fields had reverted to pasture three years earlier. IF ONLY THE PIGS COULD SPEAK!!!! What would they be telling us about the conditions in the exarable fields?

Figure 5. Recently released pigs in the rewilding project at Knepp Castle in West Sussex

Figure 6. An ancient landscaped English Park. Ancient flower and herb-rich meadows, pastures and a scatter of trees of all ages

Whilst the continuity of old trees from acorn to ancient is essential, this equally applies to our remaining landscaped parkland, meadows and pastures (Figure 6) which still remain under threat from so-called improved grassland. To date we have lost 85 percent of our ancient meadows and pastures in the last 70 yrs. This tragic loss makes the conservation of our historic landscaped parks paramount and must be considered equal to the conservation and preservation of listed houses, their contents and the gardens that surround them. Such disastrous disappearance of the flower and herb-rich meadows that were once the scene depicted in paintings of many of the famous historic landscapes. A decline in parallel with the loss of the landscaped trees started in the 1930s continued throughout the days of the Second World War up to the present day and is called grassland improvement.

Cattle can be observed more frequently now bark-stripping trees (Figure 7) and this also occurs regularly in horses and sheep. There are a number of theories as to why grazing animals do this, damaging the bark which eventually often leads to the death of the tree. One theory considered is that animals are attempting to obtain minerals, nutrients and trace elements lacking in the 'improved' grassland sward which means lack of wild flower, herb-rich roughage with the minerals, nutrients and trace elements they contain (Figure 8). The woody roughage would be a natural control on the growth of the animals' teeth. Whilst above all the fact remains that the remaining landscaped trees are under perpetual risk from browsing damage, the question remains, was the de-barking of landscaped trees still a concern before grassland improvement? Borne out by the evidence of the number of old trees that remain today, the chances are it wasn't happening.

Figure 7. Cattle bark-stripping a living tree

Figure 8. 'Real' hay – herb and flower rich

Figure 9a. Before remedial work was carried out around a tree in the public carpark at Blenheim Palace.(above) and after (below) - an excellent example of Ancient Tree care in the twenty first century

Figure 9b. The same tree after remedial work was carried out around it in the public carpark at Blenheim Palace - an excellent example of Ancient Tree care in the twenty-first century.

This ancient Oak pollard (Figures 9a & 9b) is perhaps seven hundred years old and stands in the middle of a car park at Blenheim Palace. The Palace only dates back to the eighteenth century whilst the tree could already have been three hundred years old before the first stone was laid for the building! Fortunately the tree's importance was realised by the Palace's management and a protection zone beyond the tree's canopy was extended and protected. Tens of thousands of people visit the Palace and gardens every year to admire man-made things. But how many stop and admire this tree that probably provided limbs as building timbers for the Palace? How many reflect on this tree's past? And, the history and culture that the tree has experienced and passed down the centuries beneath it's great spreading boughs. Mankind with our knowledge and experience could recreate the Palace and all it contains stone by stone but would never be able to create a seven hundred year-old Oak.

Figure 10. A landscape circle of 300+ year old lime trees in Queen Anne's Avenue in Windsor Great Park

Features in the landscape such as the circle of 300+ year old lime trees in Queen Anne's Avenue (Figure 10) which was chosen as the site for a statue in 2002 of the present Queen to commemorate her 50 years of reign, also need management to prolong their longevity. The crowns showed many signs of the trees ageing, some being very uneven and having many dead limbs prominent. There were, obviously, two opposing proposals. One to cut down, grind out the stumps and re-plant, the other to reduce the tree crowns to a uniform height and observe the outcome over time. The second course of action prevailed and the tree work has been successful and could be said to be prolonging the lives of the trees and retaining the landscape feature.

Figure 11. The Allerton Oak in Calderstones Park, Merseyside complete with the pre-war iron railing protection

The ornamental iron railings around the Allerton Oak (Figure 11) show one example of a once common feature, which not only were found throughout the many towns and cities in the UK, protecting the front gardens of dwellings but also were the boundary fences surrounding our landscaped deer parks and also protecting some individual trees, groves and roundalls. A vast proportion were removed to help the war effort during the Second World War through feeding the steel furnaces. The Allerton Oak too has its part in our nation's, and that of other nations' history because it certainly was the last old oak tens of thousands of emigrants saw as they passed on their journey to the docks and other lands across the world. These English-speaking peoples took freedom under law to the four corners of the world on ships built originally of oak.

Figure 12. Intensive sheep-grazing with some damage to ancient trees – an example of modern farming practices?

Today the old landscapers would turn in their graves to see some of these marvellous landscapes that were their vision which they went on to create but are now trashed and destroyed by modern farming practices (Figure 12). Many people in the tree world and landscape world have accepted this unnatural tragic loss of these historic landscapes and on the whole have done nothing to arrest this disaster. However, there are some examples of trees that have yet to be lost and an attempt to restore the landscape by replanting. But was the question ever asked, why they were replacing these trees and why did they die in the first place? Historic buildings and their contents and gardens have money poured into them to preserve and maintain what man has created, step out the door through the intensively, expensively manicured gardens to the historic parkland fence and view this untidy continued destruction. This complete dismissal and disregard of Brown and his contemporaries' work is not acceptable.

Bibliography

Alexander, K.N.A. (1999) The invertebrates of Britain's wood-pastures, *British Wildlife*, **11**(2), 108-117.

Green, T. (2001) Comment: Should ancient trees be designated as sites of special scientific interest, *British Wildlife*, **12**(3), 164-166.

Green, T. (2002) The role of invisible diversity in pasture landscapes. In: Redecker, B. *et al.* (eds), *Pasture Landscapes and Nature Conservation*, Springer, Netherlands.

Merryweather, J.W. (2001) Comment; Meet the glomales-the ecology of mycorrhiza. *British Wildlife*, **13** (2), 86-93.

Green, T. (2013) Ancient trees and Wood pastures. In: Rotherham, I.D. (ed.), *Trees, forested landscapes and grazing animals*. Routledge, UK.

Green, T. (2010) The importance of open-grown trees. From acorn to ancient.., *British Wildlife*, **21**(5), 334-338.

'more blackbirds than cherries' Joseph Addison

John Phibbs
Debois Landscapes

Anyone with an interest in natural history will display, with all the totemic pride that an Apache might show to his feathered headdress, an intense emotional and intellectual distaste for the works of Capability Brown. He was a man who had no interest in, and showed no knowledge of, natural history, a man who was eager to sweep it away from all the places where he worked, and who transformed the face of nature as he did so. He was like a heavy-handed picture restorer who removes half the paint in cleaning the canvas, a man, furthermore, to whose sole charge was given a National Gallery of the finest country in England.

Reasonably enough therefore, lovers of those 'little, quiet rivulets' of olde England that he did away with,[1] have for centuries dismissed his work as 'landscraping' and the man himself as a Wanton Vandal.[2]

Brown's faults are legion. He, like many of his generation, hated pollards; he planted ridiculous screens of woodland, thin enough to be known as 'belts' and far too thin to retain game, let alone wildlife; he was a lover of mono-culture; he had no problem with arable land; he substituted sullen lakes for lively streams, and above all he *improved* – though he described it as 'altering' – and his parkland was constantly described in the same terms as were applied to the improvement of waste.

He had learned as a boy at Kirkharle to clear the land of 'ponderous, massy and hard stones' and to plant.[3] His clearances at Copped Hall in about 1779 were

---

[1] Edmund Burke was concerned that all the myriad 'little, quiet rivulets' that had ornamented and watered the traditional landscape would be 'lost in the waste expanse and boundless, barren ocean' of cruelty, vulgarity, and 'homicide philanthropy' see Nigel Everett *The Tory View of Landscape* (London: Yale University Press, 1994) p.101]. In his 'Reflections on the Revolution in France' he wrote that 'all the pleasing illusions … are to be dissolved by this new conquering empire of light and reason …. To make us love our country, our country ought to be lovely' [*The Works of the Right Honourable Edmund Burke* (London: F. and C. Rivington, 1803) Vol.V pp.151-152]. The same line of thought provided him with metaphors for his great attacks on Warren Hastings' treatment of India.

[2] The word 'landscraper' was coined by Ted Green.

[3] Sir Lambton Loraine 11th Bt.*Pedigree and Memoirs of the Family of Loraine, of Kirkharle* (London: 1902) p.108, *cit.* Peter Willis 'Capability Brown in Northumberland' *Garden History* Vol. IX part 2 (1981) p.159.

reported,[4] and William Constable wrote in terms of the 'Old Thorns, old decayed forest trees, whin or gorse higher than a man on Horseback, Rushes, Hillocks, Deep Ridge and furrow, rivers and swamps' that Brown had replaced at Burton Constable.[5] In 1797, Horn wrote of Burghley that 'It was the genius of the late LAUNCELOT BROWN which, brooding over the shapeless mass, educed out of a seeming wilderness, all the order and delicious harmony which now prevail',[6] and in the same year Lord Coventry put up a casket on a pedestal by the lake at Croome with the inscription 'To the Memory of Lancelot Brown who by the powers of his inimitable and creative genius formed this garden scene out of a morass'.[7] Worse still, Steffie Shields has shown that after he left Kirkharle he was employed in Lincolnshire on drainage projects!

We natural historians read these accounts – and there are many more like them – we read them and weep.

As for Brown's treatment of pollards – he would occasionally leave them: if they were sufficiently far from the house (Moccas Court); if they were famous named trees (Langley, Bucks., Heveningham); in level sections of the parkland he, and Humphry Repton after him,[8] might use them to create a contrasting forest-like effect that would set off the elegance of his alterations (Beechwood, Haynes, Ickworth, Wakefield Lodge) or in pleasure grounds where their deformities would not be so apparent (Blenheim, Chatsworth, Petworth). Certain timbers, ships' timber in particular, could be grown on old pollards,[9] but even their commercial value was not enough to save them - for the most part they were a sick blemish on the landscape and they had to go.

---

[4] James Dugdale *The new British traveller and Modern Panorama of England and* Wales (London: 1819) Vol.II p.374.

[5] Bodleian Library English Letters 229, fol.18.

[6] J. Horn *A History ... of Burghley House* (Shrewsbury: J. & W. Eddowes, 1797) p.192.

[7] Though critical of the final effect, William Mason endorsed this opinion, 'the Water … has done great good to the Land by turning a great fen into excellent Pasture' [Correspondence between William Gilpin and William Mason, Bodleian MS Eng. Misc. d. 570 fol. 208 (29/7/1784, Mason to Gilpin)].

[8] 'where such vegetable antiquities [ravaged thorn or an ivy-covered maple] are found growing in hedge-rows above the general level of the ground, it is better to surround them with young brushwood to mass or groupe in with the other bushes, than to clear them away...' [Humphry Repton, red book for Plas Newydd, January 1799].

[9] Trees with crooked timbers were used for the 'knees' in ship-building, see N. D. G. James *A history of English forestry* (Oxford: Blackwell, 1981) p.141. Trees could be managed to provide timbers angled in certain ways. J. C. Loudon recommended this treatment for Larch which was to be turned or bent at the base: there is one superb example in the pleasure ground at Shardeloes, and a group of larches similarly treated at Heanton Satchville, see J. C. Loudon *Observations on the Formation and Management of Useful and Ornamental Plantations* (Edinburgh: A. Constable & Co., 1804) p.132; N. D. G. James *A history of English forestry* (Oxford: Blackwell, 1981) p.155.

Figure 1. Veteran Trees. Photograph taken by Joe Cornish for John Phibbs *Capability Brown: designing the English landscape* **(Rizzoli Press, 2016)**

Today's natural historian, venerating the pollard, may be taken aback by Brown's attitude. His confusion between reverence for antiquity and distaste for pollards is equally marked in the writing of the naturalist E. N. Buxton, who on the one hand saved Epping Forest, arguing in 1884 for the retention of dead and fallen trees: 'fallen giants, gorgeous with moss and lichen, and telling the story of mighty hurricanes and snowstorms that we should miss if they were removed', and on the other hand quoted with approval a report of 1864 on pollards: 'They are not, strictly speaking, trees at all, but strange, fantastic vegetable abortions. Their trunks, seldom more than a foot or eighteen inches in diameter, are gnarled, writhed, and contorted, and at about six feet from the ground, just within reach of the axe, they spread into huge overhanging crowns, from which spring branches which are cut every other year or so, and never long escape the despoiler. It is no more nature's notion of primeval woodland than are closely-cropped hair and shaven lip and chin her intention for the real expression of the human face.'[10]

Brown's response to pollards shares this complexity. He was said to require 'that every thing which indicated decay should be removed', and accordingly he 'destroyed in Blenheim park, and many other places, great numbers of the finest

---

[10] E.N. Buxton *Epping Forest* (London: Edward Stanford, 1884), *cit.* John Hunter *The Essex Landscape A study of its form and history* (Chelmsford: Essex Record Office, 1999) p.28.

studies for art that nature ever produced.'[11] It would be easy to join Uvedale Price in judging Brown to have had an aversion to pollards still more extreme than that of his contemporary designers,[12] – and it is true that many more pollards survived at parks such as Cassiobury, Windsor and Woodhall where Brown did not work.[13] However constructive advice on pollarding is hard to find in the 18th century.[14] We may admire pollards for their antiquity, for the richness of their natural history, and for their amazing and mazy structure, the product of so many wounds, so much work by untutored men of the soil over so many years, but it was precisely for those reasons that Brown condemned them.

Natural history will pass quickly – all too quickly – over the woodland belt, Brown's 'thin circular verge', so criticised by Uvedale Price,[15] 'often too long, and always too narrow ... meagre girdles of plantation, which are extended for many

---

[11] Richard Payne Knight *The Landscape* (London; G. Nicol, 1795) Part III l. 27(n). Uvedale Price's comment on the ash tree at Fisherwick is at one with his friend's response: 'what provoked me was his having prevented you from seeing, except from a single point, one of the noblest ashes I ever saw: he has not only planted about it, but has built the kitchen garden wall, or, what is only less bad, sufferd it to remain, quite close to it, so that it is impossible to enjoy what appears to be one of the finest views of this magnificent tree. I was hardly prepared for such a degree of perverse taste & judgment, though I of course could not expect from Brown or any of his followers the least variation from the established plan, "For Daisies will be Daisies still"' [Charles Watkins and Ben Cowell 'Letters from Uvedale Price (1747-1829) to Sir George Beaumont and Others, with a biography Mr Price The Picturesque: Critic, Connoisseur and Landscape Enthusiast.' *Walpole Society* Vol. LXVIII (Leeds: Maney, 2006) p.197 (to Sir George Beaumont 17th October 1806)].

[12] For 100 years of hostility to pollards, see *inter alia*, Moses Cook *The Manner of Raising, Ordering, and Improving Forrest Trees ...* (London: Peter Parker, 1676) pp.58-9; Stephen Switzer *Ichnographia rustica* (London: D. Browne, 1718) Vol.I p.259; *The letters of William Shenstone*, ed. Marjorie Williams (1939) p.252; James Wheeler *The Modern Druid, containing instructions for the much better culture of young oaks* (London: C. Davis, 1742) p.30ff ; Arthur Young *The Farmer`s Letters to the People of England* (Dublin: J.Milliken, 1768) p.256; Nathaniel Kent *Hints to Gentlemen of Landed Property* (London: J. Dodsley, 1775) p.190; *A General Dictionary of Husbandry, planting, gardening, and the Vegetable part of the Materia medica.... Selected from the Best Authorities, by the Editors of the Farmer`s Magazine* (Bath: Cruttwell, 1779; Thomas Ruggles 'Picturesque Farming', *Annals of Agriculture* Vol.VII (1786) p.23; Arthur Young *Annals of Agriculture* Vol. XVI (1791) p.509; William Marshall *Planting and Rural Ornament* (London: G. & W. Nichol, 1803; 1st ed. 1785) Vol. I pp.100-101; William Cobbett *Rural Rides*, ed. G.D.H. and Margaret Cole (London: Peter Davies, 1930) Vol.I pp.73-74 (21st January 1822; J.L.Phibbs 'Groves and Belts', *Garden History* Vol. XIX Part 2 (1991).

[13] 'A large old knotty trunk of a tree would generally be rooted up in any part meant to be improved, even at a distance from the house, much more if near it; in my idea, however, great advantage might be taken of objects of that kind, even in a pleasure ground' [Uvedale Price *Essays on the Picturesque* 3 vols. (London: J. Mawman, 1810; 1st ed. 1794) Vol.II p.139].

[14] One man prepared to discuss pollarding was Thomas Hale *A Compleat Book of Husbandry* (London: T. Osborne and J. Shipton, 1756) p.140.

[15] Uvedale Price *Essays on the Picturesque* 3 vols. (London: J. Mawman, 1810; 1st ed. 1794) Vol.I p. 244.

miles in length, although not above twenty or thirty yards in breadth'.[16] Repton himself was in no doubt about the short-comings of Brown's belts as a reserve for wildlife and found himself modifying them where he came across them: 'if the thorns were profusely scattered among the trees after the firs & Larches are taken away, it would make a better cover for game',[17] and: 'a belt of plantation ... would not be so effectual to protect the game'.[18]

Repton's mention of conifers only damns the belt still further for, above all else, Brown's belts were associated with conifers. Blenheim Park's 'utmost circumference' was fourteen miles 'round which are the most enchanting rides, shaded principally with evergreens',[19] while within the park at Holkham was 'a most enchanting ride of seven miles, in the midst of a belt of Fir and other Trees, Evergreens and Shrubs, whose Foliage exhibits a variety of Tints'.[20]

Sandys, who carried out the planting at Holkham, was a Brownian, and Nathaniel Kent claimed that the owner, Coke, had planted 'four hundred and eighty acres of different kinds of plants, two-thirds of which are meant to be thinned and cut down for underwood, so as to leave oak, Spanish chesnut, and beech, only as timber.'[21] To that account Tom Williamson's search on the ground and in the estate records at Holkham has added ash, elm and sycamore and much smaller numbers of ornamentals such as spindle, Lombardy poplar, weeping willow, Weymouth pine, plane, wild service.[22] Any natural historian will be affronted by this failure to plant indigenous species.

'... by this false [Brownian] taste for extent ... [a] great part of the interior of a park is become an arable farm'[23] Brown's attachment to arable land will win him no friends among natural historians either, but in Norfolk alone, Tom Williamson has

---

[16] Humphry Repton *Sketches and Hints on Landscape Gardening* (1795), republished in *Landscape Gardening and Landscape Architecture of the late Humphry Repton, Esq.*, ed. J. C. Loudon (London and Edinburgh: Longman & Co. and A. & C. Black, 1840) p.106.

[17] Humphry Repton, red book for Hewell Grange (25 Jan 1812).

[18] Humphry Repton, red book for Wimpole (October 1801).

[19] Rev. William Mavor *Blenheim, a poem. To which is added, A Blenheim Guide* (London: T.Cadell, 1787) p.3.

[20] J. Dawson *The Holkham Guide* (Burnham: J.Dawson, 1817) p.140. At Hewell Grange, Repton's criticism of Brown was unremitting, and his belt there was planted with 'many firs & Larches (as nurses to more valuable trees)'. These looked like 'one uniform black skreen of firs' [Humphry Repton red book for Hewell Grange (25th January 1812).

[21] Nathaniel Kent *A General View of the Agriculture of the County of Norfolk* (London: C. Macrae, 1794). p.40.

[22] Tom Williamson *The Archaeology of the Landscape park Garden design in Norfolk, England*, c.1680-1840, BAR British Series 268 (Oxford, Archaeopress, 1998) p.102.

[23] Humphry Repton *An Inquiry into the changes of taste in Landscape* Gardening (1806), republished in *Landscape Gardening and Landscape Architecture of the late Humphry Repton, Esq.*, ed. J. C. Loudon (London and Edinburgh: Longman & Co. and A. & C. Black, 1840) pp.327ff.

found eighteenth-century arable at Holkham, Kimberley, Langley, and Melton Constable.[24] Other examples from Brown's work include Alnwick,[25] Ampthill;[26] Blenheim,[27] Chilham Castle (where on 10th August 1777 Brown actually gave advice on the 'Tillage of the Ground' within the park),[28] Grimsthorpe,[29] Southill,[30] Stoke Park,[31] Stowe,[32] Syon Hill,[33] and Tatton, where Repton advised in 1792 that the low meadows, the common, the arable, and land not owned by the Egertons should be replaced by homogeneous parkland.[34] The Grove also had a relatively substantial acreage of arable (it was described as a 600-acre farm with 250 acres deer park, i.e. grassland, and it had about 100 acres of woodland).[35] Brown's deployment of arable is deservedly condemned as freely as the dreary

---

[24] Tom Williamson *The Archaeology of the Landscape park Garden design in Norfolk, England, c.1680-1840*, BAR British Series 268 (Oxford: Archaeopress, 1998) p. 99. See also Tom Williamson *Polite Landscapes Gardens and Society in eighteenth century England* (Baltimore, Maryland, Alan Sutton Publishing, 1995) pp.122-3.

[25] 'The park of Alnwick, though for the most part naked of large timber, and borrowing almost all its shade form the plantations of the last duke, offers occasionally some very fine views, as well as a pleasant ride round its boundary, which extends thirteen miles through a tract of country wisely applied to agricultural purposes, instead of being wasted in a deer-range' [Richard Warner *A Tour thro' the Northern Counties of England, and the Borders of Scotland* 2 Vols. (Bath: R.Crutwell, 1802) Vol. II p.20].

[26] Fellows and Thorpe's 1808 enclosure plan for Ampthill (Bedfordshire County Record Office, MA95 & Award Book S) has a field inside the belt called 'Ploughed Piece'.

[27] 'Let it however be observed, that at Blenheim the *ferme ornée* is combined with the magnificent park. In one quarter, the eye is delighted with the sight of waving corn, in another with green paddocks that invite the scythe: here a building dedicated to agricultural purposes, or raised for the accommodation of the necessary offices, just peeps through the deep shade of surrounding trees; there the team rattles down the slope abrupt. On one side appears a herd of deer, on another a flock of sheep, and sometimes animals native and foreign gaze in social peace...' [Rev. William Mavor *New Description of Blenheim... to which is prefixed, Blenheim, a Poem* (London: T.Cadell, 1789) pp.128-129]. Blenheim has ridge and furrow within the early park – its historian, James Bond has assumed that this was arable made within the park after it had been enclosed.

[28] 'Copies of Letters from Thomas Heron to his brother Sir Richard Heron, principal secretary to Lord Lieutenant at Dublin Castle' (Lincolnshire Archive Office Stubton VII/E/1 3 vols. Vol.I.

[29] 'At a former time I was told that [Grimsthorpe] park measured sixteen miles three quarters in circumference, and was esteemed the largest in England; since then it has, as I now heard, nevertheless, been somewhat enlarged; but different spots in it are cultivated.' ['A short tour in the midland counties of England' (1772), and 'Excursion' (1774), Bodleian Gough Gen top. 155, p.68].

[30] The 1777 estate plan, kept at the house, shows how extensive the arable was.

[31] Humphry Repton, red book for Stoke Park (2nd June 1792).

[32] In 1798 'canary, barley and pease' were grown in the Deer Park at Stowe, Huntington Library, STG estate accounts box 12 bundle 28.

[33] The Earl of Holderness grew cabbages at Syon, but in 1771 turned much or all of it to grassland, according to Arthur Young (*The Farmer's Tour through the East of England* (London: W. Strahan, 1771) Vol. IV p.85).

[34] 'This ground I have in the map called a Sheep Walk, part of it when I saw it was sown with turnips, and the rest pasture' etc. [Humphry Repton, red book for Tatton (February 1792)].

[35] See Arthur Young *A General View of the Agriculture of Hertfordshire* (London: 1804); John Claudius Loudon *Encyclopaedia of Gardening* (London: 1822) p.1233.

extent and 'lush green richness' of his grassland.[36] He was a man to add white clover to the mix when making good after earthworking, at Longleat in the 1750's,[37] at Chatsworth in 1763,[38] at Sandbeck in 1774,[39] and, very likely, whenever called upon to re-sow grassland.[40] Captain Yarranton and his ilk had had their way with him.[41]

Of his lakes, it may be sufficient to register Uvedale Price's observation that the Brownian lake was parallel-sided, with banks set at regular heights above the water,[42] when it should have had the savage quality of Claude's banks 'parts of

---

[36] For 'lush, green richness' see Woudstra & Hitchmough 'The Enamelled Mead: history and practice of exotic perennials grown in grassy swards', *Landscape Research* Vol. XXV part 1 (2000) p.37. For a contrary view, see John Phibbs *Place-making, the art of Capability Brown* (Historic England, forth-coming).

[37] '... to sow with Dutch Clover & Grass seeds or turff all such parts as shall be broke up' (Thynne Papers Box XXX Vol. LXXVII, fols.280-289). The Longleat contracts are summarised by Timothy Mowl, 'Rococo and later landscaping at Longleat', *Garden History* Vol. XXIII part 1 (1995) p.62. These contracts also show Brown using the recognised means of grassland improvement: marling, liming and drainage.

[38] John Banatt & Tom Williamson *Chatsworth A Landscape History* (Macclesfield: Windgather, 2005) p.109.

[39] Edith Milner *Records of the Lumleys of Lumley Castle*, ed. Edith Benham, (London: Bell & Sons, 1904), p.366.

[40] Brown's accounts mention 1,120 lbs. of white clover seed bought from Sambrooke Freeman for Milton Abbey, probably in 1776, suggesting that he had already used it at Fawley Court before 1771 (Dorothy Stroud *Capability Brown* (London: Faber & Faber, 1975) pp.118-9).

[41] As regards great estates, Wakefield Lodge was buying clover by the ton in 1730, and by the end of the century at the latest it was regularly being worked into the rotation, as we have seen [Michael E.Turner, John V.Beckett, Bethanie Afton *Farm production in England 1700-1914* (Oxford: OUP, 2001) p.77]. Kate Feluś has shown me the record of Brown's purchase of 45lb of clover for Stowe in 1750 (Huntington Museum, California; National Trust ID 7678 and 8291). Graham Harvey (*The Forgiveness of Nature The story of grass* (London: Jonathan Cape, 2001) pp.211-213) has a good account of early uses of clover in England from 1343. Figures for the sowing rate are hard to come by, but the Earl of Haddington planted 20 lb red clover to the Scots acre (which was 1/5 larger than the English), so Brown is likely to have been sowing around 3 acres at Stowe, see Thomas Hamilton, 6th Earl of Haddington *Forest Trees: Some directions about Raising Forest Trees*, ed. M. L. Anderson (written c1735, published Edinburgh: 1953) p.71.

[42] 'a few strokes of the painter's brush [wielded by the improver] would reduce the bank on each side to one level, to one green; would made curve answer curve, without bush or tree to hinder the eye from enjoying the uniform smoothness and verdure, and from pursuing without interruption, the continued sweep of these serpentine lines' ... 'In order ... to impress on the whole of any artificial water a character of age, permanency, capacity, and above all, of naturalness as well as variety, some degree of height and of abruptness in the banks is required. .. But as artificial lakes and rivers are usually made, the water appears in every part so nearly on the same level with the land, and so totally without banks, that were it not for the regularity of the curves, a stranger might often suppose that when dry weather came the flood would go off' [Uvedale Price *An Essay on the Picturesque as compared with the Sublime and the Beautiful* 3 vols. (London: 1810; 1st ed. 1794) Vol. I p.19, Part 2 pp. 303-304].

them covered with trees and bushes that hang over the water; and near the edge of it tussocks of rushes, large stones, and stumps; the ground sometimes smooth, sometimes broken and abrupt, and seldom keeping for a long space, the same level from, the water'.[43]

So how then are we to respond as natural historians to the fact that in spite of his apparent disdain for nature and his anthropocentricity, Brown's landscapes provide refuges for so much wildlife and host so many Sites of Special Scientific Interest?

First, we might pay lip service to the genius of Brown, while in practice working with might and main to undo all the harm he has done, and many of us do that. Second we might take the harder road and question all our assumptions in order to winnow fact from prejudice, and this is the road on which the tercentenary celebration of Brown is set.[44] But to finish, I would pick out a line of thought that may reconcile Brown the landscraper with the conservation value of the landscapes that he has left to us.

The Wallington estate consists of some 12,000 acres. It includes a number of highly designed landscapes: Liniel Law, Rothley Lakes, Rothley Castle, the *ferme ornée* and the park, besides a number of smaller features or 'diversions'. These are linked by two sets of routes – a series of public roads, so straight that they were known as turnpikes *ante diem*; and a series of informal ridings which make their way along the burns and the best scenery from one part to another. We do not know how much Brown did at Wallington, besides Rothley Lakes, but the ridings are very much in his style.

The Petworth landscape extends for around seven miles from north to south, and the 'designed' landscape covers some 3,000 acres. Brown's writ ran throughout this area though the National Trust land (deer park and pleasure ground) amounts to only about 750 acres of the whole. At North Stoneham the landscape ran up from the parkland through Rough Park to the Belvedere on the common, over about three miles. At Belvoir Castle, Brocklesby, Chatsworth, Clumber, Milton Abbey and many other landscapes, Brown was involved with 'long approaches' - private roads of up to 6 miles in length, leading from the nearly towns to the house. In short, Brown's landscapes were very extensive. His three adjacent landscapes in the Dukeries extend over 20 miles from north to south. Without writing a single management plan for newts or bats, he did create habitats that gave 'connectivity' to

---

[43] Uvedale Price *Essays on the Picturesque* 3 vols. (London: J. Mawman, 1810; 1st ed. 1794) Vol. I p. 19.

[44] Anyone who would like to engage with the community that is rethinking Brown, is recommended to consult http://thebrownadvisor.com/.

wide tracts of country and provided homes for many thousands of small animals.[45] We might learn from him a more inclusive and a more generous definition of 'environment'.

As a corollary to the great acreages over which he worked, one should add that Brown did not really do deer parks. Of course he would work with them if he had to, but where he had a choice, as at Luton, he would get rid of the deer at an early stage of the design, and where he had complete command of a project, towards the end of his career, at Belvoir Castle, Berrington, Milton Abbey, Woodchester, he would either do without deer or relegate them to a paddock outside the heart of his landscape. He reinstated the fourteenth century park at Belvoir, but described it as 'Intended Lawn to be Occasionally divided for Hay &c' and as 'The lawn with Plantations round it, to be Mowed and Fed occasionally.' – it was to be a 300-acre hay meadow.

Brown is better thought of as making farms, and indeed many of his landscapes (Adderbury,[46] Croome, Southill and Trentham were described as farms,[47] Brown himself frequently designed farms,[48] and indeed the great majority of innovative

---

[45] 'Connectivity', 'authentic', 'nature' and 'sustainable' are here given meanings that are peculiar to natural historians, and hence have been picked out by the author with inverted commas.

[46] 'A noble mansion-house, with convenient offices, fit for a large Family; together with an Old Paddock, Gardens, Pleasure Ground and other Lands, and about 224 Acres of rich Meadow, Pasture and Arable Lands, laid out for a Park, and inclosed and planted round with a Verge of Evergreens and different Sorts of Forest-Trees, all good thriving Condition, with a fine serpentine stream of Water running through the same, in full View of the House; the whole containing 278 Acres and upwards' [West Register House, Edinburgh, GD 224/89 5]. The reference to 'Meadow, Pasture and Arable Lands' is striking.

[47] For Croome, see Arthur Young *Annals of Agriculture* Vol. VI (1786) p.127; James Dugdale *The new British traveller and Modern Panorama of England and Wales* (London: 1819) Vol.IV p.517. For Southill, see the 1777 estate plan, entitled 'Plan for Wrotham Farm'. For Trentham, see James Loch A*n account of the Improvements on the estates of the Marquess of Stafford* (London: Longman, 1820) Appendix IX, where what we regard today as Trentham Park was thought of as the home farm in 1820 'The stock on the farm consists of a good flock of Leicesters, with a flock of black-faced sheep for the table. The cattle are driven up from Dunrobin... The milch cows are of the most improved Yorkshire breeds, with a proportion of Alderneys...' &c &c.

[48] Examples include Ashburnham, where the new park of about 490 acres was made by Brown on the east of the house. He turned the old park, north of the house, into farmland (see Sue Farrant 'The development of Landscape Parks and Gardens in Eastern Sussex *c.*1700 to 1820 – a guide and gazetteer', *Garden History* Vol. XVII part 2 (1989) p.176); Sledmere, where Brown proposed to enclose the sheep walks on the Wold (see David Neave and Deborah Turnbull *Landscaped Parks and Gardens of East Yorkshire 1700-1830* (Bridlington: Georgian Society for East Yorkshire, 1992) p. 65); Tixall, where the Hon. Thomas Clifford 'assisted by the taste and judgement of the celebrated Brown, and his pupil Eames ... cut off near 500 acres from the park, which he devoted to agriculture, and planted a handsome belt of wood to conceal them from the eye' [Sir Thomas Clifford, Arthur Clifford *A Topographical and Historical Description of the Parish of Tixall in county of the Stafford* (Paris: M. Nouzou, 1817) pp. 71-72]; Combe Abbey, whose historian, George

eighteenth century farm buildings were built in parkland.[49]

This observation brings me to a most painful point of self-examination, for I must now confront something that I feel and that I think others feel also, which is the snobbery of the natural historian. There is a perception, seldom directly expressed, that toothless old men, with hands as hard as boot leather and impenetrable accents, preferably pipe-smoking, are somehow the genuine article, and that their way of farming - Burke's 'little, quiet rivulets' of country life, unforced, unplanned, 'organic', handed down over the generations from the days of ridge and furrow, is somehow 'authentic' and close to 'nature'. Indeed, I have met great academics who regard the days of the open-field system as a golden age of rural life, rudely snatched away from us by the improvers of the eighteenth century. It follows from

---

Demidowicz, has found evidence that Old Lodge, and the old deer park, were turned into a farm in the 1750's. The accounts of thorn hedging that he has found suggest, as one might expect, that this was carried out over several years. What we do not have is uncontroversial evidence that the work was designed or approved by Brown, but it appears that he was party to the redivision of the farmland south of the turnpiked Brinklow road (B4027). The Gothick farm at Worksop was put up in around 1758 (see *The Yale edition of Horace Walpole's Correspondence*, ed. Wilmarth S. Lewis, 48 vols. Vol. XXXIX (London: OUP, 1955) p.48). Typical is William Gilpin's account of Cadland: 'At the small distance of half a quarter of a mile from the house, stands a most splendid farm. The stables, the cow-sheds, the pigeon-house, the graneries [sic], the barns, are all superb' [William Gilpin *Remarks on Forest Scenery* (London: R. Blamire, 1791) Vol. II p. 204]. To these one should add William Pitt at Burton Pynsent, and 3rd Earl of Hardwicke at Wimpole (his works are described in Britton and Brayley (1801-16) Vol. II (1801) pp.125-6).
Coke of Norfolk, 1st Marquess of Rockingham, 5th and 6th Dukes of Bedford, 3rd Earl of Egremont, and the 2nd Marquess of Stafford were all cited as pioneering model farmers in John Martin Robinson's seminal article ('Model Buildings of the Age of Improvement', *Architectural History* Vol. XIX (1976) p.17). All except Rockingham, and perhaps the Dukes of Bedford, used Brown.
[49] See Jeremy Lake and B. Hawkins 'Thematic listing surveys of farm buildings', *Context* Vol. LVIII (July 1998) pp.24-5. They describe model farms as 'highly inventive and influential creations' and have noted that 'the most significant developments in agricultural practice were concerned with the housing and management of animals, principally cattle, and that important new types of buildings, specifically designed for sheltering livestock, and for collecting and distributing the manure they produced' were developed from the 18th centuries. For the great barn of c1768 at Wentworth Castle, see M.J. Charlesworth 'The Wentworths family and political rivalry in the English landscape garden', *Garden History* Vol. XIV part 2 (1986) p.134. At Cadland, Gilpin regarded the 'splendid farm' with it superb stables, cow-sheds, pigeon-house, granaries, and barns, as 'too much' and tending only 'to lessen yᵉ dignity of yᵉ principal mansion' – 'As yᵉ horse is so nearly connected with his master, & contributes so much to his state, & convenience, we allow so noble an associate to lodge magnificently: as he is expected also to be ready at a call, & may be yᵉ object of attention to persons of any rank, we allow his magnificent lodging to stand near yᵉ mansion. At yᵉ same time, if it be yᵉ object of extraordinary expence, it shᵈ contribute to yᵉ magnificence of yᵉ whole, by making one of yᵉ wings, or some other proper appendage of yᵉ pile.
But for yᵉ farm, it has no title to such notice ...' [Bodleian MS Eng.misc. e. 501 Rev. William Gilpin, 'Remarks on Trees; and their several combinations; (relative chiefly to Picturesque beauty;) illustrated by yᵉ Scenes of New-forest in Hampshire: in three books' Book III of New Forest in Hampshire (Part 2). (*c.*1781) fols. 686 - 688].

this perception, which I hesitate even now to call a prejudice, that anyone (even a man of the soil, as Brown himself was) who tries to unpick that landscape in order to impose on it a more natural form of land use which is also patently anthropocentric, is necessarily behaving in an unnatural fashion and is therefore to be condemned, no matter what benefits the new management may confer.

Figure 2. Parkland Landscape. Photograph taken by Joe Cornish for John Phibbs *Capability Brown: designing the English landscape* (Rizzoli Press, 2016)

Now I realise that this idea is bunkum, but though I know it in my head, it still appeals to my heart, and I would be a hypocrite to try to uproot it from the hearts of others.

Let me finish then with the following hypothesis, which pays due respect to our toothless ancestors: Brown designed great landscapes, no matter how natural or unnatural we regard them to be, and since they are great designs, as well as stable and 'sustainable', they have survived to a remarkable degree for 250 years or more. Nothing is more beneficial for wildlife than a habitat which lasts, and the longer it lasts, in this country at least, the more diverse and rich becomes the wildlife associated with it. Therefore Brown's landscapes are closely associated with so many SSSIs, simply because he was a great designer. It follows therefore that if we look after great landscapes, nature will look after itself.

Grass, Wood and Water: approaches to the ecology of Brown's landscapes

Tom Williamson,
University of East Anglia

Brown and the Landscape Park

The essential features of Lancelot Brown's landscapes will be familiar to most readers. He famously swept away gardens enclosed by walls and hedges, avenues, and all forms of geometric planting; and in their place he created 'naturalistic' parklands, comprising wide prospects of turf, irregularly scattered with trees and clumps of woodland, and surrounded in whole or part by a perimeter woodland belt. The boundary between the mown lawns around the house, and this wider parkland landscape, was dissolved by the use of the sunken fence or *ha-ha* and, wherever topography and money permitted, a lake of serpentine or irregular form would be placed in the middle distance of the view from the windows (Stroud 1965; Hyams1971; Hinde 1986; Brown 2011; Mayer 2011; Shields 2016). None of this was entirely new. Parks, as we shall see, had existed for centuries, and purely geometric styles of garden design had been in retreat for many decades before Brown began his career as an independent designer in 1750 (Jacques 1983). Charles Bridgeman and others had, through the 1720s,created simplified geometric landscapes which already, at some places, included lakes of irregular form; and in the 1730s William Kent laid out serpentine gardens as distinct spaces within such formal frameworks, ornamented with classical buildings and scattered clumps, at Holkham, Stowe and elsewhere (Dixon Hunt 1987). During the 1740s and 50s these serpentine gardens in turn became progressively more cluttered, both with elaborate and often exotic planting, and with a whole host of weird and wonderful structures – Chinese temples, Turkish tents, gothic ruins, mosques – to create what some historians refer to as 'rococo gardens' (Mowl 1999; Symes 2011).

What was new was not serpentine landscaping *per se*, but the application of this aesthetic to the entire landscape around the house, so that the landscape of the park became its main setting, coupled with the complete rejection of all geometry. Yet Brown's style did not appear, fully-formed, at the start of his career. His early works, at places like Badminton in Gloucestershire (1752) or Ingestre in Staffordshire (1756), appear much the same as any gardens laid out at the time in a 'rococo' style, displaying a rather contrived irregularity and continuing to co-exist with geometric features like avenues. Most of Brown's energies were at this stage directed, moreover, towards the gardens and pleasure grounds in the immediate vicinity of the house, rather than at the wider landscape. By the end of the 1750s, however, one of the key features of his style had already emerged: the oft-repeated arrangement of a mansion looking down across a smooth slope of turf to a serpentine or irregular lake (Figure 1). Brown was now designing on a grander scale, moreover, and paying particular attention to drives and approaches. Geometric features like avenues were ruthlessly removed, the number of ornamental buildings was steadily reduced, and by the early 1760s all the elements of his style were firmly in place. Natural landforms, often smoothed by excavation and earth-movement were the key feature, their shape accentuated by planting and by the use of water (Williams 1983): one of the purposes of Brown's lakes was probably to highlight the topography, revealing clearly the disposition of slope and valley. Contemporary illustrations make it clear that the sides of his water bodies were kept scrupulously clear of marginal vegetation. His landscapes displayed a serpentine simplicity: they were almost abstract and minimalist in form.

Figure 1. Kimberley, Norfolk, showing the classic Brown design feature of an expanse of smooth turf extending uninterrupted from house to water

One important feature, not always sufficiently emphasised, were the carefully tended grass rides, and gravelled drives, which threaded through the parkland, and ran in and out of the perimeter belts (Figure 2). Earlier styles of 'naturalistic' garden had privileged particular views and prospects, and they had employed features and buildings to convey messages, ideas and emotions. In Brown's parks the landscape itself - the massing of trees, the disposition of water and the shapes of landforms -

was the message. His designs were meant to be experienced on the move, along the rides and drives, on horseback or in a carriage - and thus as a continuum, rather than primarily as a succession of distinct experiences. Thomas Whateley's lengthy description, written in the late 1760s, of the approach to Caversham in Berkshire (laid out by Brown a few years before) captures this concept well, one section describing how:

> The road passes between the groups [of trees], under a light and lofty arch of ash; and then opens upon a glade, broken on the left only by a single tree; and on the right by several beeches standing so close together as to be but one in appearance; this glade is bounded by a beautiful grove, which in one part spreads a perfect gloom, but in others divides into different clusters, which leave openings for the gleams of light to pour in ... (Whateley 1770, 148).

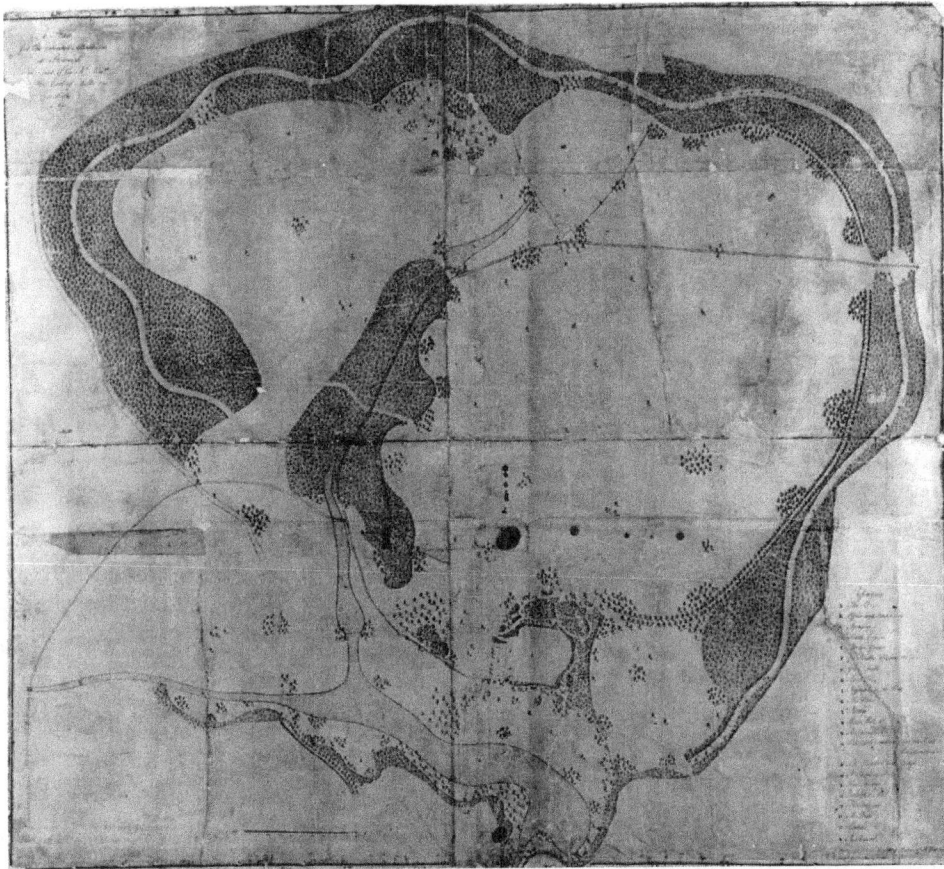

Figure 2. Bowood, Wiltshire: Brown's plan of 1763 is perhaps the earliest to show all the features of his fully developed style. Note the complex lake; the approach from the south (right), across two bridges; circuit ride; perimeter belt; and extensive pleasure ground. All of this was laid out at the expense of a working agricultural landscape

The landscape was thus a continuous if varied whole, less like a series of static pictures than the words and punctuation in a sentence, as Brown himself explained in a conversation he had with Hannah More in 1782:

> He told me he compared his art to literary composition. "Now *there*", said he, pointing his finger, "I make a comma, and there," pointing to another spot, "where a more decided turn is proper, I make a colon; at another part, where an interruption is desirable to break the view, a parenthesis; now a full stop, and then I begin another subject (Roberts 1836, 237).

It seems that he employed this analogy regularly: the *Gazetteer and New Daily Advertiser* for 1780 described how the planting of a single willow had been Brown's sole contribution to the grounds of Garrick's villa in Hampton, and noted:

'This single addition Brown compared to punctuation, and not without some felicity of phrase, called it a dot, the presence and operation of which, as it were, made sense of the rest'.

Brown was not of course the only designer working in England in the second half of the eighteenth century, creating simple parkland landscapes like this. He must have been responsible for significantly less than a tenth, and probably less than a twentieth, of the landscape parks which existed by the time of his death in 1783. Several other people, including Nathaniel Richmond, Richard Woods, Thomas White, John Davenport and Samuel Driver, ran businesses which similarly worked on a national scale. Woods, for example, is known to have undertaken at least 45 commissions, mainly in the area around London and in Yorkshire (Cowell, 2009); Richmond designed at least 30 gardens and landscapes (Brown, 2000). In addition to such regional or national practices, innumerable provincial land surveyors and nurserymen provided fashionable landscapes, often of great subtlety and beauty, the local gentry. It is often assumed, nevertheless, that Brown invented this familiar style and that other practitioners were mere 'imitators'. Yet there is no real evidence that this was so. Brown's early designs for places like Badminton or Ingestre appear no different from the plans prepared by contemporaries like the Greening brothers or Francis Richardson in the early or mid 1750s; his more developed style of the 1760s seems much the same as that practised by men like Driver, Woods or Richmond. Rather than being invented by one man, the 'landscape' style was simply the fashion of the times, developed as a collaborative affair by a broad group of designers, many of whom knew each other personally (Brown and Williamson, 2016). It came to be associated so closely with Brown because he was its most commercially successful practitioner, operating a complex and sophisticated business and scooping up the richest and most influential clients.

That business, moreover, did not only supply sweeping parkland. It also provided elegant pleasure grounds, shrubberies and flower gardens, for in spite of what critics were beginning to assert even before the eighteenth century was over, Brown never really left the mansion standing 'solitary and unconnected' in a vast sea of grass. At Lowther (1771) amongst other places his plan marks the 'site for the flower garden'; at Kimberley in 1778 the main feature of the design was a long, narrow ribbon of pleasure ground which extended all the way from the house to the lake; while at one of his final commissions, Heveningham in Suffolk (1782), a visitor in 1784 described a flower garden immediately to the east of the house (Scarfe 1988, 141). Failure to supply an area in which flowers and shrubs could be displayed would have been odd, given that this was a period in which new plants from America and elsewhere were eagerly acquired by the wealthy (Laird 1999). Brown and his team also supplied architectural services, providing designs for rebuilding, extending or modernising around twenty country houses, as well as for new stables, ice houses, and services buildings – at Kimberley in Norfolk Brown's plan even shows a new 'drying yard' for the washing. He supplied menageries (places where collections of exotic animals were kept and displayed) and numerous kitchen gardens. And as well as providing lakes, Brown frequently installed complex systems of land drainage, ensuring that the area in the immediate vicinity of the mansion, the sweep of turf between it and the lake, and the various rides and paths threading through the park, were all kept suitably dry. Brown at one point described himself, rather aptly, as a 'place-maker', who provided 'all the elegance and all the comforts that Mankind wants in the Country' (Stroud 1965, 157).

Deer Parks and Landscape Parks

All this said, it was the sweeping landscape of the park, complete with clumps, lake, and network of rides and drives, which was the most distinctive contribution of Brown and his fellow designers. Parks were not, of course, invented in the eighteenth century. They were a long-established feature of the English landscape (Fletcher, 2011; Liddiard, 2007; Mileson, 2009). Deer parks originated in the early Middle Ages as enclosed and private wood-pastures, used as hunting grounds and venison farms, which were often located at a distance from the mansion (Figure 3). During the late Middle Ages their numbers declined: the economic dislocations of the fourteenth century placed considerable strains on demesne incomes, while rising wages and the decline of customary services ensured that maintenance costs spiralled. But more importantly, parks were now more closely associated with residences, for as they dwindled in numbers, the survivors were usually among the relatively few examples that had been located beside great houses. And as the numbers of parks began to increase once again through the fifteenth and sixteenth centuries, these new creations were, almost without exception, similarly placed. There were changes, too, in their appearance. Early medieval parks had been densely-wooded, usually with relatively few open areas or 'laundes'. But as parks were brought into closer association with the residence they tended to become more open in appearance, and their layout and design came to be more carefully considered. The number of trees within them was reduced, for otherwise the house would have been hemmed in by woodland - and it would not have been possible to demonstrate the wealth of an owner who was able to put vast acres out of cultivation to create a landscape devoted, ostensibly, to leisure. This said, sixteenth and seventeenth-century parks generally remained, in essence, wood-pastures, densely filled with pollarded trees as much as timber. A survey of Hatfield Middle Park in south Hertfordshire, made in 1669 recorded 1,613 pollards of oak (*Quercus robur*) and beech (*Fagus sylvatica*) within the park itself and a further 72 growing on the bank of the park pale: but in addition, 255 values are given for hornbeam (*Carpinus betulus*) pollards, each said to represent 40 trees, suggesting that that there were, in all, 10, 133 pollards growing on the park's 350 acres, a density of around 70 per hectare (HHA, Hatfield House General 47/28).

Figure 3. Staverton Park, Suffolk – a densely-treed wood-pasture - conveys a good impression of the appearance of a medieval deer park

From the middle of the seventeenth century parks began to be wrapped around the mansion and its gardens, and in some places the boundary between it and the wider world was hardened with the planting, along the line of the perimeter fence or pale, of a thick belt of trees. And, in the last decades of the century – for a few brief decades, lasting into the early eighteenth – the geometric design of the garden was extended out into the park in the form of avenues and other geometric planting, although these constituted intrusions into the park's natural informality, rather than a radical displacement of it. Long before the arrival of 'Capability' Brown the park was thus a distinct form of landscape, designed to varying degrees and with an immense pedigree, loaded with significance and meaning. As Oliver Rackham has emphasised, Brown and his contemporaries were the 'heirs to a long tradition': the eighteenth century was simply the period in which the design of parks 'became an art form' (Rackham 1986, 126-8; Rackham 2006, 139-41).

Figure 4. Heveningham Hall in Suffolk, as depicted in William Watts' ***The Seats of the Nobility and Gentry*** **of 1786, with carriages running across the smooth turf of Brown's park, and a boat sailing on his lake. The parkland is much more open, and much less densely-planted, than would have been the case in earlier wood-pasture parks**

All this said, one of the dangers in landscape studies, as in historical ecology, is that we confuse terms and things. Often, in Rotherham's words, 'to ecologists, a park is a park' (Rotherham 2012, 4); yet while there were continuities in the development of parks, there were also important discontinuities, so that 'park' meant rather different things in different periods. Eighteenth-century parks were not only much more open and more carefully planted than earlier parks. They were also tidier, more manicured in appearance; they were sparsely scattered with timber trees, not densely filled with pollards. They were landscapes of clean lines, of serpentine minimalism, their aesthetic closely associated with new 'Neoclassical' fashions in architecture, with their emphasis on planes, simplicity, and on distinct, continuous outlines rather than on the complex, fussy forms of the rococo, or the rugged and broken lines beloved of later 'picturesque' designers (Figure 4). Brown would surely have shared the enthusiasm of contemporary Neoclassical architects like Robert Adam for the simple and the 'pure', their rejection of 'superfluous ornament' and above all their belief that architectural forms were to be derived from nature's beauties, distilled through examination and abstraction. For Brown, landscaping was not a matter of ephemeral fashion or whim, but of systematic observation and the application of appropriate enhancements. In his own words:

> Place-making, and a good English Garden, depend intirely upon Principle and have very little to do with Fashion, for it is a word that in my opinion disgraces Science wherever it is found (Stroud 1965, 157).

Brown's parks did not, therefore, very closely resemble the grazed wood-pasture of the traditional deer park. Brown and his contemporaries took an ancient symbol of elite status and provided it with a fashionable makeover – gave it an elegant veneer more suited to the age. As Thomas Whateley put it in 1770, gardening was 'no longer confined to the spots from which it borrows its name, but regulates also the disposition and embellishments of a park …' (Whately, 1770, 1).

One clear sign of this is the declining importance of deer in parks. They had been their original *raison d'etre*, and as late as 1750 most people would have thought of parks as enclosures in which deer were kept: county maps continued to depict parks as circuits of deer-proof fencing well into the 1760s. But by this stage the connection between deer, and parks, had been loosened, and during the following three decades many existing parks lost their deer, while new parks – and large numbers of new ones were created in this period – were usually grazed by sheep and cattle alone. Indeed, one of the key achievements of Brown and his fellow designers was to divorce the concept of the park from any necessary association with deer. At some of the places where Brown worked his canvas was an existing deer park, and deer continued to be kept there by his clients, as at Petworth or Sledmere. But many of his commissions, such as Shortgrove, Broadlands or Croome, involved creating entirely new park landscapes, which were grazed by domestic livestock alone. By the end of the century only a relatively small minority of parks contained deer. In part this change reflects the fact that landscape parks proliferated from the 1750s and descended the social scale: by the end of the eighteenth century even quite minor landowners could boast their own 'park', but would have been unable to find the money required to maintain a deer-proof fence. But the separation of the two concepts – deer, and parks - was also associated with the fact that deer are voracious grazers, difficult to keep out of clumps and shrubberies. The more elaborately planted parks became, the less they could be used for venison farming. In short, Brown's parks owed something to traditional wood-pasture parks, but the differences between the two were probably as great as the similarities. In their developed form, Brown's landscapes were above all displays of tidiness and simplicity, in which natural landforms were exposed by sweeping prospects of turf, and enhanced and highlighted by the use of planting and the creation of lakes.

The impact of these three key elements – turf, wood, and water - on biodiversity and wildlife are best considered in turn. But before we do so it is necessary to make an important distinction between the *immediate* ecological effects of park-making in the eighteenth century, and the longer-term impacts, as these landscapes matured and eventually grew old. In addition, we need to distinguish benefits accruing from the entirely new features and habitats created by eighteenth-century park-making – plantations, lakes and the like: and those which resulted from the way that these eighteenth-century parks retained and re-used existing features of the landscape, such as farmland trees and ancient woods. When eighteenth-century designers talked about the need to consult the 'genius of the place' when laying out parks and gardens, they were thinking, not only of paying careful attention to the character of the natural landforms, but also of the measured re-use of features like these already existing in the landscape.

Turf

Today, surviving parklands are often valued as islands of relatively unimproved pasture within what are otherwise intensively farmed landscapes, characterized by a herb-rich sward and, in many cases, much disturbance by moles, ant hills and the like. But their importance in this respect, and the extent of the contrast with the surrounding landscape, would generally have been less marked in the eighteenth and nineteenth centuries, when parks were still young. Although the kinds of seed mixes available to park-makers were less monocultural in character than those employed in (for example) modern playing fields; and while Brown himself often included clover in the mix; large-scale grassing down of former arable fields would have produced, initially, relatively uninteresting swards. The dominant aesthetic of smooth, close-cropped turf, designed to enhance the subtlety of landforms, should also be noted here: the areas of parkland close to the house, at the very least, will have been kept tidy and clear of molehills, fallen branches, disturbance and the growth of weeds like thistles, for large landowners did not lack the labour to undertake such necessary maintenance. We need to remember the 'manicured' character of these landscapes: and the charactersiation of Brown, once a taste for a rougher form of nature began to develop in the last decades of the century, as the the 'Thin, meagre genius of the bare and bald', and the widespread assertion the 'monotony and baldness are the greatest defects of improved places' (Knight 1794; Price 1794).

It is true that in the arable east of England, especially, large areas of open grass, even like this, would have provided some refuge for mammals and birds displaced from local pastures by the shift to more intensive arable husbandry which was occurring in the second half of the eighteenth century, and from the neighbouring commons by enclosure. It is also true that, whether managed by grazing or mowng, being generally immune from ploughing and re-seeding, they would within a few decades have grown floristically rich, and often remain so today if they have not been subject to twentieth-century re-seeding or herbicide applications. The Great Lawn at Chatsworth, although created slightly earlier that Brown's time (it was probably laid out by William Kent in the 1730s), is a good example of how time can transform biodiversity (Barnatt and Williamson 2005, 50-73). No less than 56 species of angiosperm have been recorded here, including many not normally thought of as inhabiting lawns, such as tormentil (*Potentilla erecta*), milkwort (*Polygala serpyllifolia*) and yellow mountain pansy (*Viola lutea*) (Gilbert 1983). It was, however, the *long-term* rather than the immediate impacts of emparking which were crucial.

This said, we should also note that in many cases parks were laid out over ancient pastures and meadows – land which had always been used as grassland or, more usually, land which had been enclosed from open fields some time during the previous three of four centuries, and laid to grass. The ridge and furrow preserved beneath the parkland turf in Brown's parks at places like Chatsworth in Derbyshire or Burghley in Cambridgeshire had usually been fossilised, by the laying of arable to pasture, many decades or centuries before the creation of the parks themselves. Almost always, because both reflect an absence of later arable land use, archaeological and biological interest go hand in hand.

In short, newly created pastures will have had some environmental benefits, and will then have acquired species gradually, over time; ultimately achieving in many places a high degree of floristic diversity because they were generally farmed less intensively that surrounding land, and less likely to be subject to reseeding and, in more recent decades, herbicide and fertilizer applications. But at the same time, parks were important for their role in preserving pastures already old and biologically diverse.

Lakes

The lakes created by Brown and his fellow designers were arguably their greatest contribution to ecology. Ignoring the 'meres' of Shropshire and Cheshire; the similarly named lakes in parts of East Anglia; and the 'broads' in the same region; very few water bodies of any size actually existed in lowland England at the start of the eighteenth century. There were, it is true, some substantial fish-ponds in late medieval and early post-medieval deer parks, which were occasionally almost lake-like in their dimensions, but nothing to compare in scale to the water bodies created in the eighteenth century by Brown and his fellows. But these men did not invent lakes as a feature of designed landscapes for they were already being created on some scale in the larger parks through the 1720s and 30s, by or under the influence of designers like Charles Bridgeman and William Kent. In the county of Norfolk, for example, lakes had, by the 1740s, already appeared in the parks at Raynham, Holkham, Gunton, Wolterton and Houghton (Williamson 1998). In 1739, even as Brown was leaving his native Northumberland and heading south to Stowe, one contributor to *The World* was able already to mock the current trend for 'moving earth', and the way that 'a Serpentine River and a Wood are become the absolute Necessities of Life, without which a gentleman of the smallest fortune thinks he makes no Figure in the country' (Richardson 2007, 125). All this said, the numbers of lakes unquestionably increased dramatically in the second half of the eighteenth century.

As well as being novel impositions on alien landscapes, eighteenth-century lakes were unnatural in other respects, often being highly engineered. Few were excavated into the ground to any significant extent: like earlier fish ponds, they were essentially created by ponding back the waters of a stream, or river, behind dams. The latter were often complex features, usually incorporating devices to allow the lake to be emptied for maintenance as well as mechanisms to control the outward flow of water: water levels needed to remain relatively constant throughout the year, and provision needed to be made for spates after heavy rain. Brown's contract for Melton Constable in Norfolk in 1764 typically stipulated that he should supply the dam with 'a proper plug'; that for Petworth in 1756 bound him to 'make a proper plug and Trough to draw down the Water, as likewise a Grate for the discharge of waste water'; while that for Bowood noted that there should be 'Plugs, Grates and wastes for the discharge of floods' (NRO, Seaton Delavel acquisition EW 21; WSRO, PHA/6623; Bowood archives). Many of Brown's lakes had an ornamental cascade on the lower side, as at Charlecote; others, as at Fisherwick, were disguised as 'sham bridges'. Some of Brown's dams, like those of his contemporary designers, had a thick layer of clay on the lake side, covered by a pitching of stones; but sometimes there was a thick central core of clay, especially where the lake had to support the heavy rockwork of a cascade on the lower side (Roberts, 2001). How often the sides and base of the lake were 'puddled' – lined with rammed clay – is unclear. It is often assumed that this was normal practise but there are few unequivocal references to it in the surviving documents, and most lakes, located on flood-plains, probably held water reasonably well without it. At some places, such as Kimberley in Norfolk, by-pass channels were provided to reduce silting (contemporaries were as aware as modern owners of the problems caused by the inflow of sediment, one describing how the construction of Brown's lake at Peper Harrow in Sussex 'will be attended with some difficulty to secure it from choking by the sands that are continually washed down') (ESRO AMS 6185/242). Some of the more complex lakes, as at Bowood, seem to have been provided with small but separate water bodies at their upper ends, retained by small dams or slip ways, which could act as silt traps. Even so, most eighteenth-century lakes suffered from some degree from silting, and have had to be dug out on a number of occasions in their history – an expensive operation which few modern owners can afford. Brown's lakes were created out of dry land, and to dry land most will eventually return.

Many eighteenth-century parkland lakes today function as County Wildlife Sites or Sites of Special Scientific Interest, such as that at Eridge Park on the Kent/Sussex border. But in terms of their environmental benefits, we need once again to distinguish between immediate and long-term impacts. When first constructed, eighteenth-century lakes were, to judge from contemporary illustrations, kept scrupulously free of marginal vegetation, in keeping with the minimalist, manicured character of the wider landscape (Figure 5). Being directly connected to an existing watercourse, they would have soon been colonised by aquatic vegetation and fish, as well as used by waterbirds, but their real importance for wildlife perhaps only really developed in the course of the nineteenth and twentieth centuries, firstly as new fashions allowed a measure of marginal vegetation to develop, and especially as many parkland slid into a state of poor maintenance during the first half of the twentieth century, leading to the development more extensive beds of reeds and the like.

Figure 5. Brown's magnificent lake at Castle Ashby, Northamptonshire, still has clean sides, without marginal vegetation

Plantations and Trees

The third great contribution made by Brown and his contemporaries was the addition of many thousands of trees to the landscape, mainly in clumps and plantations, but also scattered across the parkland turf. Planting could be on a truly monumental scale. At Chatsworth, for example, 10,000 oaks and 15,0000 mountain ash and birch were purchased and planted in the new plantations in the park in 1760 alone, in addition to an uncertain number of trees grown on the estate itself (Barnatt and Williamson, 2005, 112). At Holkham in Norfolk the belts and clumps planted in the last decades of the eighteenth century contained more than two million trees. Looking today at the over-mature remnants the plantings made by Brown and his contemporaries, it is only with an effort that we remember that these were once young trees. Indeed, contemporaries often emphasised the intended rather than the actual impact of planting, Lady Shelburne thus describing Brown's plantations at Bowood in Wiltshire in 1765 as 'very young but promising' (Bowood archives: Lady Shelburne's Diary, Vol 2, 12). The planting in parks formed part of a wider enthusiasm for forestry which had been developing since the late seventeenth century. Landowners were fired up by the writings of men like John Evelyn, whose book *Sylva, or a Discourse on Forest Trees* of 1664 was followed by a rash of similar texts, including Moses Cook's *The Manner of Raising, Ordering and Improving Forest Trees* of 1676 and Stephen Switzer's *Ichnographica Rustica* of 1718. Planting was a patriotic duty, for there was widespread concern that there was a general timber shortage which had implications for the nation's naval power, as writers like Phillip Miller (1731), James Wheeler (1747) and William Hanbury (1758) all warned. In a more general sense the planting of trees demonstrated confidence in the new political dispensation brought about by the Restoration of the Monarchy, and by the Glorious Revolution of 1688 (Daniels 1988). But planting was also carried out to beautify estates, and to provide cover for game. In the course of the eighteenth century progressive improvements in gun technology made it easier to shoot game in the air, rather than on the ground. At the same time, enclosure and the consolidation of land into larger and more continuous properties, both critical developments of the eighteenth century, allowed game to be more carefully preserved (Munsche 1981, 8-27). Shooting accordingly became more organised and competitive, with shoots involving larger numbers of participants, leading to the more systematic management and encouragement of game, and to an increasing focus on the pheasant as the principal quarry of sportsmen in lowland areas. Unlike other kinds of game bird, the pheasant occupied relatively small territories, could thus be raised in large numbers, and was easily scared into flight, making it an excellent target (Hopkin 1985, 68). But because it is a woodland bird, large areas of new woods needed to be planted to provide it with a congenial environment (Delabere Blaine 1838, 854; Hill and Robertson 1988, 38-45). There is little doubt that by the time of Brown's death the woods and clumps of the landscape park were, on most estates, well stuffed with pheasants. As William Marshall said of Norfolk in 1787:

> Ornamental plantations, about the residences of men of fortune, are here, as in other districts fashionable: not, however, as objects of ornament merely, but likewise as nurseries of game (Marshall 1787, I, 120-1).

Some of the parkland clumps, and belts, were evidently coppiced, like traditional woods. Where they were not, they were – like most new plantations of the period – planted very densely with timber trees, usually at intervals of around a metre. They contained the long-established mainstays of estate woodland, like oak (*Quercus* sp.) and elm (*Ulmus* sp.), but also sweet chestnut (*Castinea sativa*), beech (*Fagus sylvatica*) and sycamore (*Acer pseudoplatanus*), indigenous or naturalised species which were now planted way beyond their earlier ranges. These were mixed with a rather larger number of 'nurses', most of which were conifers, especially larch (*Larix decidua*) and Scots pine (*Pinus sylvestris*). In the words of the agricultural writer Nathaniel Kent, plantations in Norfolk consisted of 'Great bodies of firs, intermixed with a lesser number of forest trees' (Kent 1796, 87). The trees were very densely planted and then repeatedly thinned, starting with the softwoods, and then removing a percentage of the hardwoods. How useful plantations like this were as habitats in the short or medium term is unclear: intensive and regular thinning, coupled with the activities of gamekeepers, may have ensured that that they were less important for wildlife then than they often are today, in an over-mature state. Individual trees were retained for longer in parkland plantations, because they were managed for aesthetics more than their monetary value, than they were in traditionally-managed woods – thus providing in time an abundance the kinds of micro-habitat associated with only over-mature specimens. Not surprisingly, a number of woods planted in eighteenth-century parks are now important local nature reserves. Even when first planted the smaller woods and belts probably benefited the more common farmland birds, and provided habitats for a number of woodland species, including the red squirrel.

Where parkland belts were originally coppiced, in the traditional manner, they can today sometimes closely resemble ancient, semi-natural woodland, not least because some have been quite extensively colonised by the 'indicator species' supposedly characteristic of such woodland (dogs mercury (*Mercurialis perennis*), wood anemone (*Anemone nemorosa*), primrose (*Primula vulgaris*) and the rest), at least where they planted beside ancient hedges which acted as reservoirs for such species. In Norfolk, for example, the woods planted along the perimetre of Gawdy Hall Park in Harleston some time between 1734 and 1783 (and now known as Blake's Grove, Ladies' Grove and New Grove) are all included in the *Ancient Woodland Inventory*, in spite of their relative youth (Barnes and Williamson 2015, 171-4) As with other features of the landscape park, the biological importance of woods and belts increased with the passing decades and centuries, as these comparatively undisturbed environments grew to maturity and beyond.

Figure 6. A detail from Brown's second design for Kimberley in Norfolk, 1778, showing the planting by the lake. Weeping willows, conifers, and what may be Carolina poplars are depicted. This is an extreme case, but many of Brown's plans show some exotic or coniferous planting

The passing of time modified parkland planting in other ways. We often assume that the individual trees scattered across the turf of Brown's parks were dominated by indigenous or naturalised specimens, and it is clear that oak, elm and beech, together with sweet chestnut and common lime, were the most common specimen trees planted in eighteenth-century parks. But much use was also made of exotics such as London plane (*Platanus × acerifolia*) and evergreen oak (*Quercus ilex*), as well as of a wide range of conifers, principally Scots pine, spruce and larch. Close examination of Brown's plans often shows such trees scattered across the parkland turf, as at Kimberley in Norfolk; or grouped into clumps, as at Wimpole in Cambridgeshire. The same approach was evidently adopted by other designers and Mason, writing in 1768, suggested that the 'greatest fault of modern planners is their injudicious application of *Fir-trees. –* A quick growth and perpetual verdure have been the temptations for introducing them; but these advantages are very insufficient to justify the prevailing mode, which gives them universal estimation' (Mason 1768). Conifers were also used to vary the margins of Brown's perimeter belts, as at Burton Constable in Yorkshire, where the minutes of meetings held between him and the estate's agent, Robert Raines, have survived (Hall, 1995, 170). Here the planting, almost certainly in the park rather than the pleasure grounds, included sugar maple (*Acer saccharum*) and scarlet oaks (*Quercus coccinea*), while other trees which – while indigenous - we would today perhaps associate more with gardens rather than parkland were widely established, most notably silver birch (*Betula pendula*), which were purchased in their thousands. Weeping willows (*Salix babylonica*) are often shown on Brown's plans, gracing the margins of his lakes or rivers (Figure 6). The comments of eighteenth-century visitors often suggest a more varied palette of planting than we generally assume. At Brown's Peper Harrow in Sussex it was noted by one that in the low ground by the lake – some way from the house – 'the plants in general grow remarkably well, especially the Americans which require bog earth' (ESRO AMS 6185/212). Most of the conifers and ornamentals used by Brown and his contemporaries not only grow fast, however: they also die young, and to some extent this has served to accentuate the indigenous, 'natural' character of eighteenth-century planting. The cedars of Lebanon (*Cedrus libani*) which often survive – and which are sometimes described as Brown's 'signature tree' (Brown 2011, 89) - represent the long-lived tip of a rather larger iceberg which has vanished, leaving the longer lived oaks, sweet chestnuts, beeches and limes: making Brown's parks appear, in a sense, more like the ancient wood-pasture deer parks which were their partial model. The elms so widely planted in eighteenth-century parks were, sadly, all lost to disease in the 1960s and 70s; but other planting, where it survives, has sometimes reached 'veteran' status – especially the beech trees, which seldom attain an age of more than three centuries, so that those planted by Brown are generally approaching the end of their natural life.

Once again, we see how parks have become more ecologically important and diverse over time. But in the case of planting, also of importance is the way that emparking served to fossilise, and re-use, existing features of the landscape, sometimes already very old. Previous areas of woodland constituted one of the raw materials out of which eighteenth-century parks were shaped. Vistas and prospects could be sculpted from continuous areas of woodland, as for example at Ashridge in Hertfordshire, where the 'Golden Valley' to the north of the house was created by removing trees at the base of a dry Chiltern valley and leaving the woodland, with carefully scalloped margins, on the upper valley sides. It is still a stunning sight (Figure 7) (Leiper 2012, 92-120). At Langley in Norfolk Brown's activities, in the mid-1760s, included the expansion of an existing deer park at the expense of Langley Wood, an area of ancient semi-natural woodland, which lay immediately to the north (Fenwick 2016). Brown's plan shows that the wood was to be thinned, to leave an abundance of free-standing trees; sections were retained to form clumps (Figure 8). More usually, such densely-planted areas – whatever their origins – formed a more distant backdrop to the main area of parkland; and existing woods, often of some antiquity, were connected by additional planting to form the perimeter belt, the shape and extent of the park thus emerging from the hints provided by the existing landscape. Alexander Pope had earlier described how the joining of 'willing woods' was one important aspect of consulting the 'genius of the place' (Davis 1978, 316). At Bowood, to take one example, much of the perimeter belt shown on Brown's plan of 1763 already existed, as discrete blocks of woodland interspersed in the fields, on an estate map made in that same year. As late as 1805 a survey of the park was still distinguishing between the 'old woods' and the 'plantations' made at the time of Brown (Bowood House archives).

Figure 7. Brown's 'Golden Valley' at Ashridge in Hertfordshire was carved out of a more continuous tract of woodland pasture

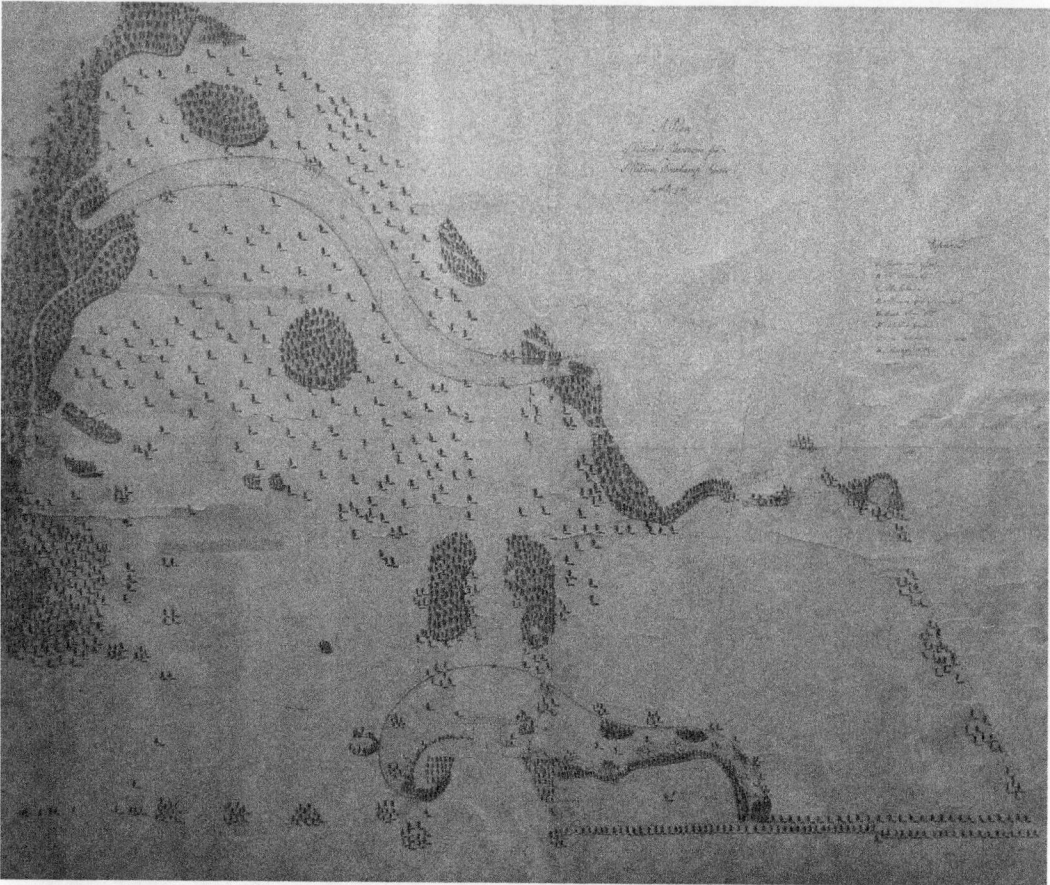

Figure 8. Brown's plan for Langley in Norfolk, 1765. The north-western section of the park is, unusually for one of Brown's parklands, densely-timbered: the trees have been left behind when the rest of the ancient Langley Wood was removed

Veteran Trees

In ecological terms, perhaps the most important features of eighteenth-century parks are the ancient trees they often contain, and the opportunities these provide for saproxylic insects and other important wildlife. It is sometimes assumed that such trees are a feature of eighteenth-century parks because many or even most of these evolved from medieval deer parks; and that these in turn were normally enclosed from early medieval grazed woodlands which had themselves developed, without interruption, from the natural wood-pasture landscapes of remote prehistory. In Keith Alexander's words, 'medieval wood pastures lent themselves to enclosure as deer parks, which became the landscape parks of Brown's schemes' (ancienttreeforum.co.uk/saproxylic-beetles-in-capability-brown-landscapes-and-the-importance-of-continuity/). Looked at in this way, eighteenth-century parks represent direct lineal descendants of the prehistoric 'wildwood'. But we need to be extremely careful here. Early medieval parks, because of they were enclosed from the dwindling remnants of the wooded 'wastes', tended to be located towards the margins of parishes and townships; they had therefore often been abandoned even before the fashion for 'residential' parks developed in the late Middle Ages. The latter were usually, although not invariably, laid out around long-existing manor houses in areas anciently farmed and settled: they were thus usually created out of cultivated land, their makers accordingly retaining existing hedgerow trees to provide the necessary sylvan prospects. Already, designers of parkland were consulting, as their eighteenth-century successors were to do, the 'genius of the place'. Some of these late-medieval or early-modern parks did evolve into the landscape parks of the eighteenth century, but a very high proportion did not, for many great houses were abandoned, and new ones created, as the fortunes of particular families and estates waxed and waned over the centuries. In short, the idea that *most* eighteenth-century parks developed into the eighteenth-century parks landscaped by Brown and his contemporary designers, while frequently asserted, has less often been demonstrated, and appears inherently unlikely.

Closer inspection confirms such scepticism, although it must be emphasised that England boasts very varied regional landscapes, with very varied histories, and different districts clearly display varying degrees of continuity between primeval woodlands and eighteenth-century parks. In Norfolk, for example, it is extraordinarily hard to find any probable examples. Of the 119 landscape parks which existed in the county by the 1790s, probably only two or three had certain medieval origins (Williamson 1998, 40-6). Of these, Hunstanton was certainly a late medieval creation, made at the expense of previously cleared ground; but Melton Constable (where Brown worked) probably developed directly from a park created in the thirteenth century from an area of wooded waste, although this is not certain. Kimberley is a more complex example. The medieval mansion of Wodehouse Towers stood on a moated site within a deer park, created in the fifteenth century, in Kimberley parish, some way to the west of the present Kimberley Hall - which actually stands on the eastern side of the river Tiffey, in the parish of Wymondham. This latter mansion was erected in the early eighteenth century by Sir John Wodehouse, 4th Baronet, and set within a new deer park. There was no continuity at all with the medieval park: the two lay in different places and their areas did not overlap until the subsequent expansion of the new park, in the eighteenth and nineteenth centuries (Taigel and Williamson 1991, 69-71). Even if we include Kimberley, less than 2 per cent of eighteenth-century parks in the county appear to have originated as early medieval deer parks, carved out of the primeval 'wastes'. Hertfordshire makes an interesting comparison. It was particularly well-endowed with parks in all periods, in part because of an abundance of woodland and in part because of its proximity to London. To judge from a comparison of the particularly complete corpus of medieval deer parks compiled by Anne Rowe (Rowe 2009), and the depiction of parks on the Ordnance Survey Draft Drawings of 1799-182 in the British Library, there was here rather more continuity. Of the 153 parks of various kinds in existence in c.1800, 18 (12 per cent) overlie, in whole or part, medieval deer parks. However, only in eight cases (5 per cent) does there appear to have been *direct* continuity, with deer park evolving into eighteenth-century park: in others, there seems to have been a period of discontinuity, in which disparking was followed by a period of agricultural use, before the areas in question were emparked once again, in whole or part. In Shropshire, to judge from the research of Sandra Morris, there were rather more examples of long-term continuity: probably around 9 of the 64 parks (14 per cent) existing in 1752 originated in the Middle Ages, although at least three of these were probably late medieval creations, laid out at the expense of agricultural land (Morris 2015, 64). But in Northamptonshire, most eighteenth-century parks clearly – from both archaeological and cartographic evidence – overlie medieval arable land. Only 7 per cent developed in the early Middle Ages, or were enclosed in more recent times, from woodland or wood-pasture within one of the three royal forests of Rockingham, Salcey or Whittlewood.

Figure 9. Veteran oak trees, several with medieval origins, stand on the earthworks of a lost roadway within Brown's park at Kimberley in Norfolk

This is not to deny that *some* eighteenth-century parks developed directly from deer parks with medieval origins. The fine collections of veteran trees in some of Brown's landscapes, at Blenheim in Oxfordshire for example, originated in early wood-pastures. But in most cases the presence of ancient trees, and saproxilic insects, cannot be explained in this way. Wimpole Park, for example, which Keith

Alexander implies is an example of such continuity (ancienttreeforum.co.uk/saproxylic-beetles-in-capability-brown-landscapes-and-the-importance-of-continuity/), cannot be so, for the entire park overlies the earthworks of abandoned medieval settlements and open fields – in the Middle Ages, its entire area was under cultivation, largely without hedges, and with only one small area of woodland (RCHME 1968,225-9).

Ancient 'veteran' trees, especially oaks, are indeed common in landscape parks but the majority originated as farmland trees, mainly growing in hedges, which were preserved when the park was first laid out (Rackham 2004). The fine collection of medieval oaks in Kimberley Park, for example, lie well outside the area of the former medieval deer park and most are clearly associated with the earthworks of field boundaries (Figure 9). The same is true of the huge oak pollards, with their nationally important lichens and bryophytes, in the parks at Benacre or Sotterley in Suffolk, both of which appear to be post-medieval creations, laid out over enclosed farmland (Ratcliffe 1977, 116; Williamson 2000, 80-81; 84). A few examples of ancient trees in parks, such as the fine hornbeam pollards at Woodhall in Hertfordshire, probably originated in areas of wood-pasture, but not in deer parks: these particular trees seem to have originally grown on a wooded common. But in most cases, old trees in eighteenth-century parks originally grew as pollards in farmland, and not in deer parks or other ancient wood-pastures. It is these, rather than wood-pastures as usually conceived, that must have formed the vector of continuity for organisms dependent on ancient trees. Emparking provided one link in a complex chain of biological continuity.

Discussion

The idea that the elegant parklands of eighteenth-century England usually represented the direct, lineal descendants of primaeval 'forests' has an emotional appeal, but it is over-simple. It also obscures a number of other, more interesting stories, and directs us away from more intriguing questions. One concerns why, precisely, such a high proportion of veteran trees are to be found in landscape parks – in some areas, almost all examples. There is good evidence that, from an early date, people in general found old trees appealing (Barnes and Williamson 2011, 131-5). But for the most part trees were regarded in practical, economic terms and were managed accordingly. Few timber trees, on farmland or in woods, probably lived much beyond their seventieth year and, while pollards continued to be productive into old age, even they would usually be taken down as they became seriously old, for it was better to chop them up and burn them on the fire, and get a young tree started in their place, than to depend on an increasingly meagre crop of poles for fuel. It is a miracle that any trees reached advanced senescence in the fuel-hungry world of early medieval England (Warde and Williamson 2014). Their chances of survival were obviously much greater, however, where they became a feature in a landscape laid out around the home of a wealthy individual who could indulge in the luxury of their retention, valuing them for their appearance and antiquity rather than for the wood or timber they afforded.

Another, rather bigger question concerns the character of biological 'continuity', which the 'landscape park as ancient wood-pasture' model arguably treats in too simplistic a manner. The presence of saphroxilic insects in parks does not, as the example of Wimpole so clearly demonstrates, necessarily indicate unbroken continuity of tree cover from remote prehistory. Populations of such insects can evidently be wiped out from particular areas only to be re-establish themselves from neighbouring locations – the kind of 'shifting continuity' posited by Rotherham and others in their discussions of ancient woodland (Rotherham 2012). Indeed, by rejecting simple models of on-site continuity we can arguably learn far more not only about these particular insect species, but about long-term biological processes in the landscape more generally.

References

Abbreviations for archives consulted
NRO - Norfolk Record Office
Bowood archives - Bowood House, Wiltshire, examined with permission of Lord Lansdowne.
HHA – Hatfield House archives.
ESRO – East Suffolk Record Office.
WSRO – West Suffolk Record Office.

Secondary Sources
Barnes, G. & Williamson, T. (2011) *Ancient Trees in the Landscape: Norfolk's Arboreal Heritage*, Windgather Press, Oxford.

Barnes, G. & Williamson, T. (2015) *Rethinking Ancient Woodland: the Archaeology and History of Woods in Norfolk*, University of Hertfordshire Press, Hatfield.

Barnatt, J & Williamson, T. (2005) *Chatsworth: a Landscape History*, Windgather Press, Macclesfield.

Delabere Blaine, P. (1838) *An Encyclopaedia of Rural Sports*, London.

Brown, D. (2000) *Nathaniel Richmond (1724-1784) – 'One of the Gentleman Improvers'*, unpublished PhD thesis, University of East Anglia.

Brown, D. (2001) Lancelot Brown and his associates. *Garden History*, 29, 2-11..

Brown, D. & Williamson, T. (2016) *Lancelot Brown and the Capability Men: Landscape Revolution in Eighteenth-Century England*, Reaktion, London.

Brown, J. (2001) *The Omnipotent Magician: Lancelot 'Capability' Brown*, Chatto and Windus, London.

Cook, M. (1676) *The Manner of Raising, Ordering and Improving Forest Trees*, London of 1676

Cowell, F. (2009) *Richard Woods (1715-1793): Master of the Pleasure Garden*, Boydell, Woodbridge.

Daniels, S. (1988) The Political Iconography of Woodland in Later Georgian England'. In: Cosgrove, D. & Daniels, S. (eds) *The Iconography of Landscape: Essays on the Symbolic Representation, Design and Use of Past Environments*, Cambridge, Cambridge University Press, 43-82.

Davis, H. (ed.) (1978) *Pope: Poetical Works*, Oxford University Press, Oxford.

Dixon Hunt, J. (1987) *William Kent, Landscape Garden Designer: an Assessment and Catalogue of his Designs*, Victoria and Albert Museum, London.

Evelyn, J. (1664) *Sylva, or a Discourse on Forest Trees*, London.

Fenwick, M. (2016) Langley. In: Bates, S. (ed.) *Capability Brown in Norfolk*, Norfolk Gardens Trust, Aylsham, 65-99.

Fletcher, J. (2011) *Gardens of Earthly Delight: the History of Deer Parks*, Windgather Press, Oxford.

Gilbert, O. (1983) The ancient lawns of Chatsworth, Derbyshire, *Journal of the Royal Horticultural Society*. 108, 471-4.

Hall, E. (1995) ''Mr Brown's Directions": Capability Brown's landscaping at Burton Constable (1767-82)', *Garden History*, 23, 145-174.

Hanbury, W. (1758) *An Essay on Planting*, London.

Hill, D. & Robertson, P. (1988) *The Pheasant: Management and Conservation*, RSP Professional Books, Oxford.

Hinde, T. (1986) *Capability Brown: the Story of a Master Gardener*, Norton, London.

Hopkins, H. (1985) *The Long Affray*, Faber, London.

Hussey, C. (1967) English Gardens and Landscapes 1700-1750, *Country Life*, London.

Hyams, E. (1971) *Capability Brown and Humphry Repton*, Dent, London.

Jacques, D. (1983) *Georgian Gardens: the Reign of Nature*, Batsford, London.

Kent, N. (1796) *General View of the Agriculture of Norfolk*, London.
Laird, M. (1999) *The Flowering of the English Landscape Garden: English Pleasure Grounds 1720-1800*, University of Pennsylvania Press, Philadelphia.

Langley, B. (1728) *New Principles of Gardening*, London.

Leiper, H. (2012) Mr Lancelot Brown and his Hertfordshire Clients. In: Spring, D. (ed.) *Hertfordshire Garden History, a Miscellany, II: Gardens Pleasant, Groves Delicious*, University of Hertfordshire Press, Hatfield, 92-120.

Liddiard, R. (ed.) (2009) *The Medieval Park: New Perspectives*, Windgather Press, Macclesfield

Marshall, W. (1787) *The Rural Economy of Norfolk*, London.

Mayer, L. (2011) *Capability Brown and the English Landscape Garden*, Shire, Princes Risborough.

Mileson, S. (2009) *Parks in Medieval England*, Oxford University Press, Oxford.

Miller, P. (1731) *The Gardener's Dictionary*, London.

Morris, S. (2015) *Shropshire Deer Parks c.1500 - c.1914 Recreation, Status and Husbandry*, unpublished PhD thesis, University of East Anglia.

Mowl, T. (1999) *An Insular Rococo: Architecture, Politics and Society in Ireland and England, 1710-70*, Reaktion, London.

Munsche, P.B. (1981) *Gentlemen and Poachers*, Cambridge University Press, Cambridge.

Payne Knight, R. (1794) *The Landscape: a Didactic Poem in Three Books, Addressed to Uvedale Price Esq.*, London.

Price, U. (1794) *Essay on the Picturesque, As Compared with the Sublime and the Beautiful*, 3 Vols, London.

Rackham, O. (1986) *The History of the Countryside*, Dent, London.

Rackham, O. (2006) *Woodlands*, Collins, London.

Rackham, O. (2004) Pre-Existing Trees and Woods in Country-House Parks, *Landscapes*, 5, 1-15.

Ratcliffe, D. (1977) *A Nature Conservation Review, Vol I: the Selection of Biological Sites of National Importance to Nature Conservation in Britain*, Cambridge University Press, Cambridge.

Richardson, T. (2007) *The Arcadian Friends: Inventing the English Landscape Garden*, Bantam, London.

Roberts, W. (1836) *Memoirs of the Life and Correspondence of Mrs Hannah More*, London.

Roberts, J. (2001) Well tempered clay: constructing water features in the landscape park, *Garden History*, 2(1), 12 -28.

Roberts, W. (1836) *Memoirs of the Life and Correspondence of Mrs Hannah More*, London.

Rotherham, I.D. (2012) Searching for Shadows and Ghosts. In: Rotherham, I.D., Handley, C., Agnoletti, M. & Samojlik, T. (eds) *Trees Beyond the Wood: an Exploration of Concepts of Woods, Forests and Trees*, Wildtrack Publishing, Sheffield, 1-16.

Rowe, A. (2009) *Medieval Parks of Hertfordshire*, University of Hertfordshire Press, Hatfield.

Royal Commission on Historical Monuments (RCHME) (1968) *An Inventory of the Historical Monuments in the County of Cambridge*, Volume 1, West Cambridge. London, HMSO.

Scarfe, N. (ed.) (1988) *A Frenchman's Year in Suffolk: French Impressions of Suffolk Life in 1784*, Boydell, Woodbridge.

Shields, S. (2016) *Moving Heaven and Earth: Capability* Brown's *Gift of Landscape*, Unicorn Publishing, London.

Stroud, D. (1965) *Capability Brown*, Country Life, London.

Switzer, S. (1718) *Ichnographia Rustica*, 3 Vols., London.

Symes, M. (1991) *The English Rococo Garden*, Shire, Princes Risborough.

Taigel, A. and Williamson, T. (1991) Some early geometric gardens in Norfolk, *Journal of Garden History*, 11(1) & (2).
Turnbull, D. (1990) *Thomas White (1739-1811): Eighteenth-Century Landscape Designer and Arboriculturist*, unpublished Ph.D thesis, University of Hull.

Warde, P. & Williamson, T. (2014) Fuel supply and agriculture in post-medieval England, *Agricultural History Review*, 62(1), 61-82.

Whateley, T. (1770) *Observations on Modern Gardening*, London.

Wheeler, J. (1747) *The Modern Druid*, London.

Williams, R. (1983) Making places; garden-mastery and English Brown, *Journal of Garden History*, 3, 382-5.

Williamson, T. (1998) *The Archaeology of the Landscape Park: Garden Design in Norfolk, England, c.1680-1840*, British Archaeological Reports, Oxford.

Williamson, T. (2000) *Suffolk's Gardens and Parks: Designed Landscapes from the Tudors to the Victorian*, Windgather Press, Macclesfield.

Capability Brown 'in Europe'; the nature of the 'English landscape garden'

Jan Woudstra
University of Sheffield.

Abstract

Capability Brown did not set out to improve biodiversity, or ecological habitats, nor did he set out to create nature. His landscapes were cultural landscapes, in order to achieve specific land management objectives, created according to contemporary aesthetic standards, which were open to interpretation to those able to look and see.

On the European continent, the Brownian landscape has been variously interpreted as liberation from the *ancien regime* and a symbol of the Enlightenment. These landscapes were believed to represent a return to nature, *retour a la nature,* or so it was expressed by the philosopher Jean Jacques Rousseau, who had spend considerable time in England studying them. On the continent the outlandish fashion left the issue of the origins in doubt and in the event it became the *jardin anglos-chinois* or the *jardin pittoresque.* The latter was a reference to painters of natural scenery who supposedly had provided the inspiration for the new style. In Britain it was not until the final decade of the eighteenth century until this became the Picturesque garden, inspired by natural scenery, or 'real nature'. Till then, in accordance with Brownian principles, and those attributed to the *jardin anglos-chinois,* the composition of planting was formulaic and based on early eighteenth century planting principles of the *bosquet a l'angloise.* Here widely spaced plants were graduated according to height in mixed schemes, with this principle being applied to plantations, as well as shrubberies and flowerbeds.

The flowering of what became the 'English' landscape garden on the continent was not until the nineteenth century, and while graduated planting remained generally adopted, this coincided with the existence of the more difficult to manage picturesque types of arrangement. In both instances however the general layout celebrated artifice –a distinction between art and nature was purposely sought- with artificial serpent shaped lakes, mounding and contouring, and above all stencil-like layouts of walks that over time became more contrived in order to achieve a profound caricature of naturalness. Ultimately all this was ridiculed and rejected by twentieth century modernists, who sought real nature, not in visual appearance, but in substance, i.e. in the presence of native plants and animals. This new attitude, supported by official policies of biodiversity and nature conservation, caused historic English landscape gardens to be managed as natural resources rather than the cultural landscapes they are. Over the years this has caused not only a deterioration of the historic fabric, but also degradation of biodiversity as exotic plants were exterminated. It is only in the past fifteen years or so that the English landscape garden was literally being rediscovered, with names of long forgotten designers emerging. What this meant with respect to the planting has not really been appreciated, and restorations often concentrate on recreating the configuration of walks and creating some open spaces. It will be a while yet before the essence of the Brownian garden really sinks in.

Introduction

The creation of gardens is revealing of man's relationship with nature, with the Brownian landscape, i.e. the English landscape garden, being interpreted as a closer, more intimate, relationship. On the European continent however the English garden was considered as exotic, and in the term to describe them, the *jardin anglos-chinois* –the Chinese English garden- its true origin clearly was not understood and confirms that this was seen as foreign. It did not become the English 'landscape' garden, until after Humphry Repton, one of Brown's successors, popularised the concept of landscape gardening. It is this change of name that has gradually affected perception of the English landscape garden, from exotic to the native. This paper reveals how in over two centuries the English garden has become a vehicle of the 'landscape-like', the indigenous, and how this has affected the treatment of historic parks as a result.

Eighteenth century perceptions of nature

When the Frenchman Pierre-Jean Grosley visited England in the 1770s, Capability Brown was in his heyday. Yet instead of focusing on a landscape designed by him, Chiswick House was on the itinerary. This had been one of the most influential gardens of the first half of the eighteenth century, where Lord Burlington had re-created a Classical garden. Initially this had a rather formal layout with straight hedge lined avenues, but also containing contrived serpentine walks in the wilderness area. This layout was gradually transformed by opening wider views through removal of hedges, while still leaving a regular framework of avenues in place, and as a result had become referred to as being the birthplace of the landscape tradition. After Burlington's death the garden became slightly overgrown, but clearly retained its reputation as an early landscape garden with Grosley writing in *A Tour to London* (1772), that: 'It is from wild uncultivated woods, that is, from pure nature, that the present English have borrowed their models in gardening.'

He remarked that: 'The great avenues of their parks, kept in the best order, are roads cut through forests of trees of all sorts and sizes.' So instead of regular plantations of the same shape and size in the French manner, there was a mix of tree species and sizes. He continued: 'The foot ways imitate little paths of woods by their sinuosities, and their manner of intersecting and communicating with each other', so now it becomes evident that the sinuous paths represented something more natural, which was also conveyed in the manner of planting:

> Art scarce displays itself at all in the different plantations which separate and conceal these walks: it lies in the choice of the trees and shrubs. Daisies and violets, irregularly scattered, form the borders of them. These flowers are succeeded by dwarf trees such as rose-buds, myrtle, Spanish broom, etc. The next row are filled by cedars, pines from different parts of America, and other trees which rise only to a certain height, or whose growth is very slow: the last stage consists of trees capable of forming the highest and best furnished stems. By means of this arrangement these plantations exhibit the trees in their several ages, in the pyramidal form, that is to say, the form most pleasing to the eye. The paths which they separate, and by which they are bordered, are little winding alleys, that never run the space of two fathom upon the same line, or the same plan. In laying out these gardens, the object of the first labour is the inequality of the ground, which is gained even on the levellest surface, by digging into, and removing the earth.[1]

It is clear that this is not the type of arrangement we would now recognize as nature, but was in fact graduated planting that after being invented at Kensington Palace in the first decade of the eighteenth century as the centre piece for a wilderness, had evolved to the standard and proper manner of planting shrubberies in the pleasure grounds of landscape gardens, including those designed by Brown. It was not till the latter decade of the eighteenth century that a new, a picturesque, manner of planting started to evolve, but the graduated manner that came to be identified with the early landscape gardens on the continent, remained popular throughout the nineteenth century. Those laid out on a pleasure grounds scale were either referred to as *jardin anglos-chinois*, or as romantic gardens, were of much smaller scale than the extensive Brownian parks. The thrust of these landscapes was rather of an exotic nature.

One of those who had taken on the picturesque manner of planting as a preferred way, was Prince Pückler Muskau in his *Hints on Landscape Gardening* (1834). He promoted landscape gardening within the context of the 'higher cultivation of the pleasures of life' noting that England had 'also developed it into the most delightful pursuit for the friend of Nature, for the connoisseur who loves her most when she appears in unison with the shaping hand of man, as the raw jewel first obtains its greatest beauty only through polish'.[2] Here it is clear that man was there to perfect

---

[1] M[onsieur] Grosley in *A Tour to London or New Observations on England and its Inhabitants* (London, 1772), p.116

[2] Prince von Pückler-Muskau, *Hints on Landscape Gardening* (Boston and New York: Houghton Mifflin, 1917), ed. Samuel Parsons, p.4

nature, and throughout the subsequent period the notion of art and nature became intertwined.

Copying nature

One of the most notable features that illustrates this relationship between art and nature were lawns that were normally created either through turfing, i.e. removal with a turfing iron of sheep grazed grass from selected locations – often from 'heathland'– brought to gardens. These would normally contain the finer grasses, and be virtually weed free, creating the type of tight cut lawn for which the English had been famous since the early seventeenth century. Another method was to sow areas with grass seed from selected locations; this was normally hayseed, collected from stacks, and varied hugely in species composition, depending on location, and besides grass normally included a substantial amount of flowers. This was a more economical way for more extensive areas, but instead of a pure lawn-like character would normally have provided a flower rich sward.

Flower rich swards had been appreciated in Western culture since the classical era, and which in designed landscapes normally included so-called enamelling, the planting of exotic species within the meadow. This traditional practice was also generally applied on the continent in landscape parks, with a late example being Hermann Jäger, who in his influential *Lehrbuch der Gartenkunst* (1877), recommended that copying of nature was the only rule in order to achieve flowering meadows. He recommended planting of both native and exotic plants, with the latter located near walks and seats. Areas that were to be maintained as closely mown lawns were recommended for naturalisation of spring bulbs, such as crocus, *Scilla, Ornithogalum, Muscari*, daffodils, snowdrops, snowflakes, winter aconite, wood anemone and *Corydalis*. It would be possible to mow these at the first spring cut. In long grass meadows he recommended amelioration with red and blue flowers since native meadows contained mainly white and yellow flowers. Native plants that might be added to provide a more lively appearance included *Jasione, Phyteuma, Salvia*, various geraniums, *Trifolium rubens* and *Vicia*. Exotic plants were selected on whether they grew well in meadows and flowered till hay time. These included *Sisyrinchium anceps, Filipendula rubra, Dicentra spectabilis, Trollius, Papaver bracteatum, Pyrethrum roseum, Lithospermum pulchrum, Achillea nobilis, Achillea ptarmica flore pleno, Hemerocallis* and *Lupinus perennis*.[3]

Landscape as prototype

Historical assessments of the landscape style have tended to identify them in romantic and landscape styles, with little to distinguish them. One example of this is C.L.J. Schaum, a Boskoop teacher, who in his 1915 history noted that the English

---

[3] Hermann Jäger, *Lehrbuch der Gartenkunst* (Berlin: Hugo Voight, 1877), p.442

landscape was copied as accurately as possible, on a smaller scale, and that the composition of scenes created were determined by the rules of painting. Here the notion of 'nature' had been transposed for the 'English landscape'.[4] This was further nuanced by Pannekoek and Schipper, in the 1974 edition of their standard text book for landscape architecture, where they suggested that the inspiration for the landscape style was the English landscape, especially that along the Thames, with its large number of meanders and remnant meanders.[5] It is clear that the emphasis now was on an understanding and interpretation of the term landscape style, rather than a more philosophical basis, which by this time had rather separated man (culture) and nature.

On the continent the forms to which the landscape style had evolved during the second half of the nineteenth century, to stencil like layouts, were now considered both out of place and not purposeful. They were seen as excesses that needed to be rationalised. In the meanwhile a more scientific understanding of nature had led to the possibility of reproducing habitats in new layouts, such as by Erwin Barth in Sachsenplatz, Berlin-Charlottenburg, or Jacobus Thijsse in Thijsse's hof, Bloemendaal, both in the 1920s. These projects included the regional plant communities and specifically excluded exotic plants. In Germany, but also in The Netherlands, this movement towards more scientific approaches with respect to vegetation had a tremendous influence on landscape architecture. It affected the layout and management of greenspace in towns, 'landscape-like' approaches to planting in the countryside, and also the treatment of cultural landscapes. Many of the historic landscape parks were gradually submitted to new standards of management and maintenance that no longer respected the historic intentions of the layouts. As these parks matured exotic trees and shrubs were gradually weeded out or not replaced, and if replacement took place it was normally with native varieties in line with the landscape-like character of the layout.

Conclusion

The English landscape garden was not a term that would have been recognized by Brown, yet his methods of layout and planting made an important contribution to it. Elements such as parks and belts, pleasure grounds with shrubberies, drives and walks, lawns and lakes, were all important features that he first pioneered and which then became standard components of the English landscape garden. It contained exotic plants, as well as natives in arrangements that were clearly contrived. At the time these gardens were presented as an expression of nature in which the contribution of man was valued as an enrichment of it. In the twentieth century, the landscape garden became interpreted as an expression of the English landscape. The change of understanding of these landscapes had significant impact

---

[4] C.L.J. Schaum, *Geschiedenis der Tuinkunst* (Zwolle: Tjeenk Willink, 1916), p.117-

[5] Pannekoek and Schipper, *Tuinen: Tuin-Park-Landschap* (Amsterdam: Kosmos, 1974), p.48

on the general treatment, the management and maintenance. The maintenance of English landscape gardens has tended to adopt countryside practices, in use of equipment and techniques, which in many cases is affecting the general fabric, the infrastructure and management of planting. Many parks have seen significant reduction in shrubby vegetation, and there has been a substantial reduction in exotic plants, as ones that have died have not been replaced, and others have purposely been removed in a drive that favoured native vegetation. This course of treatment is affecting not only the remaining historic fabric or cultural grain, but also the biodiversity, in restricting it in both quality and quantity.

Shorter contributions

Historic designed landscapes - an undervalued resource? - an overview of ecosystem services with focused research on ecology, connectivity and landscape character at Capability Brown sites
Leslie Pearman, Natural England

Historic designed landscapes (HDL) contribute many environmental benefits yet remain an undervalued resource. Natural England reports on two research projects that support this concept and makes suggestions for further action.

The National Character Area ecosystems framework identified many of the environmental opportunities HDLs can provide. A study of 25 HDLs, including five Brown Sites, identified those parkland features that contributed to ecosystem services and highlighted their significance to genetic diversity; climate, water quality and water flow regulation; sense of history and place and biodiversity. Data collected from 130 Brown HDLs demonstrated their importance for biodiversity. Collectively they support 12 of the 18 BAP priority habitats, five of which occurred within the Brown Sites at least double the density of that found in the surrounding landscape, as did ancient and replanted ancient woodland, broadleaved, mixed broadleaved and mixed coniferous woodland and surface water bodies. Of the Brown Sites 42% were partly or wholly within a SSSI.

Further analysis demonstrated that ecological connectivity within Brown sites is generally high while connectivity to the wider landscape is not. HDLs offer an oasis for biodiversity in intensively managed agricultural landscapes.

****

Capability Brown and beyond – Petworth Park, West Sussex
Crispin Scott, National Trust

Petworth Park, West Sussex is a 276-hectare deer park owned and managed by the National Trust. "Capability" Brown was commissioned by 2nd Earl of Egremont to work on the site between 1751 and 1763. Most of the land and the historic mansion came to the National Trust in 1947 from Lord Egremont's descendants, who still live on the property and continue to be involved in managing the park, deer and surrounding estate.

Ecological surveys of the park in recent years have revealed its importance for a range of wood pasture specialists from bats (16 of the UK's 18 species identified) to veteran trees, saproxylic invertebrates, lichen and fungi to pond specialists and solitary bees in park walls. This presentation will summarise the importance of this Brownian landscape for biodiversity and pose some questions about the challenges for the park's ecology as we look to the next 250 years. How can we address issues such as potential increases in visitors, climate change, new pathogens and the need for financial and environmental sustainability, and what are the potential benefits for the park's ecology from the National Trust's new Vision for a land that is: healthy, beautiful, rich in culture and nature, enjoyable and productive?

****

Sustaining the lichen legacy of parkland trees
Tim Wilkins, Natural England

A look at why ancient and veteran trees in parkland are a treasure-trove for lichens and the huge challenges we face conserving this interest in future. Historical attrition of lichen species has led to many becoming rare or restricted in their range. Today over 50 parkland species are listed as conservation priorities in England and yet face the emerging threats of new tree pests and pathogens, air pollution and climate change. What will the future hold for parkland lichens and how can we make populations more resilient?

Chatsworth Park, June 2016 © Christine Handley

Visit our website: www.ukeconet.org for further information
The South Yorkshire EcoNet
Wildtrack Publishing, Venture House, 103 Arundel Street, Sheffield S1 2NT